NANCY HARRIS

Nancy Harris is an award-winning playwright from Dublin.
Theatre credits include *Two Ladies* (Bridge Theatre, London);
The Red Shoes (Gate Theatre, Dublin); *Our New Girl* (Bush
Theatre, London/Atlantic Theater, New York); *No Romance*
(Peacock Theatre, Dublin); *Love In A Glass Jar* (Peacock Theatre,
Dublin); *Baddies: The Musical* (Unicorn Theatre, London);
Journey to X (National Theatre Connections); *The Kreutzer
Sonata* (Gate Theatre, London/La Mama, New York).

Nancy received the Rooney Prize for Irish Literature and
the Stewart Parker Award for her debut full-length play
No Romance in 2012. She was a finalist for the Susan Smith
Blackburn Award. She has also written for radio and television
and was nominated for a BAFTA as a Breakthrough Talent in
2014 for her writing on the Channel 4 series *Dates*.

Other Titles in this Series

Nancy Harris

THE BEACON

NICK HERN BOOKS
London
www.nickhernbooks.co.uk

A Nick Hern Book

The Beacon first published in Great Britain in 2019 as a paperback original by Nick Hern Books Limited, The Glasshouse, 49a Goldhawk Road, London W12 8QP

The Beacon copyright © 2019 Nancy Harris

Nancy Harris has asserted her right to be identified as the author of this work

Cover design: Anne Fleming and Johanna DeGreew

Designed and typeset by Nick Hern Books, London
Printed in the UK by Mimeo Ltd, Huntingdon, Cambridgeshire PE29 6XX

A CIP catalogue record for this book is available from the British Library

ISBN 978 1 84842 882 9

Woodland
CARBON
www.woodlandcarbon.co.uk
NICK HERN BOOKS
Printed on Carbon Captured paper

The Beacon was produced by Druid and the Gate Theatre, Dublin, and first performed at the Town Hall Theatre, Galway, on 20 September 2019, before transferring to the Gate on 2 October 2019. The cast was as follows:

DONAL	Ian-Lloyd Anderson
BEIV	Jane Brennan
BONNIE	Rae Gray
RAY	Dan Monaghan
COLM	Marty Rea

Director	Garry Hynes
Set and Costume Designer	Francis O'Connor
Lighting Designer	James F. Ingalls
Sound Designer	Gregory Clarke
Fight Director	James Cosgrave

Acknowledgements

My heartfelt thanks to Garry Hynes, for commissioning this play, for believing in it and for her great patience while she waited for me to deliver it.

Huge thanks also to Selina Cartmell for her continued support and encouragement and for bringing *The Beacon* so wholeheartedly to The Gate's stage.

My thanks also to the following people, who in various ways were instrumental to the development of this play: Marty Rea, Rory Nolan, Mallory Adams, Catherine Byrne, Thomas Conway, everyone at Druid, everyone at the Gate Theatre, Dave Evans, Rochelle Stevens, my family. And lastly, to Kwasi, with love.

N.H.

For Dad, with love

Characters

BEIV, *late fifties, early sixties, from Dublin*
COLM, *thirties, from Dublin*
BONNIE, *twenties, from California*
DONAL, *thirties, from West Cork*
RAY, *twenties, from South Dublin*

Note on Text

A forward slash (/) indicates an overlap in dialogue.

Setting

Beiv's cottage on an island off the coast of West Cork.

Modern, stylish, minimalist.

The back wall is made almost entirely of glass and looks out onto the sea.

On one side of the room is a front door. A beaded curtain leads out to a kitchen, off.

This text went to press before the end of rehearsals and so may differ slightly from the play as performed.

ACT ONE

Scene One

BEIV, COLM *and* BONNIE.

BEIV *sits in an armchair on one side of the room.*

BONNIE *and* COLM *are on the other on the sofa – suitcases by their feet.*

A huge canvas covered in predominantly red, pink and purple paint stands on an easel between them.

BONNIE *is looking at the canvas.*

BONNIE. You can really see the female rage. Like I'm instantly getting menstrual blood, the blood of childbirth, genital mutilation, haemorrhaging – pretty much all female suffering. Abortion is in there obviously… and repression and shame. But there's also something really – tender too. Like there, in those softer shades, I see the vulva. And the clitoris, and this really female desire for pleasure, for sexual intimacy but also for like a really fucking explosive orgasm, you know…

She laughs.

COLM *shifts, uncomfortable.*

But yeah. No, it's powerful. And brutal. And sad too.

BEIV *nods, then looks at the canvas, taking in* BONNIE*'s assessment.*

BEIV. It's a blood orange.

BONNIE *looks at her, confused.*

BONNIE. A blood –

BEIV. Orange. Still a work-in-progress obviously and the colours are magnified and exaggerated. /

BONNIE. Oh /

BEIV. But yeah. It's an orange.

Beat.

BONNIE. Wow.

BONNIE *looks at the canvas again.*

I see so much more.

COLM. Well that's art for you.

COLM *gets up to look around.*

Bonnie loves all that bullshit. (*To* BEIV.) Show her the prints of your womb series. (*To* BONNIE.) She did them around the Repeal the 8th. They're blobs basically but people saw all sorts, tears, fetuses, surgical implements. You wouldn't fucking believe the shit people will read into blobs.

BEIV (*dry*). He has a poet's touch, doesn't he, Bonnie?

COLM. Well I'm just not into beating around the – bush, or whatever. Pardon the… show her… (*To* BONNIE.) You'll love them.

BEIV. I don't have them with me.

COLM. Thought you took everything?

BEIV. I'm not dragging every feckin canvas I ever painted down here, am I? Don't have the room for a start. Not till I have a proper studio.

COLM. So where are they?

BEIV. In Dublin. In storage. A gallery in New York is interested so.

BONNIE. Wow. That's great.

BEIV (*weary*). I dunno.

BONNIE. It's not a good one?

BEIV. Oh it's a good gallery alright. I'm just getting a bit old for all this… traipsing round the world with my wares.

COLM. She's scared of planes.

BEIV. No –

COLM. Developed a fear of flying in recent years.

BEIV. That's not true.

COLM. Were you not taking those herbs?

BEIV. Ah feck /

COLM. Rescue Remedy or whatever?

BEIV. That stuff's a cod.

BONNIE. Works for me.

BEIV. Not for me. Not for the kind of thing I was suffering.

BONNIE (*concerned*). You were suffering?

BEIV. I'm grand now, don't worry about it. I just don't have the energy for all the schlepping round any more.

COLM. You didn't mind it when Dad was here.

BEIV. No.

COLM. Very fucking happy to schlep all over the world then, being lauded. Ireland's great feminist artist.

BEIV (*wry*). Do you think he's bitter about his childhood, Bonnie?

COLM. Just stating fact.

BEIV. I'm not Ireland's great feminist artist.

COLM. Who is then?

BEIV. Fuck knows, I don't keep up with this stuff. Will anyone have more tea?

BONNIE. Yes please.

BONNIE *holds out her mug.*

BEIV *starts to pour it from a teapot.*

COLM *looks around.*

COLM. Like what you've done with the place.

BEIV. What have I done with it?

COLM (*to* BONNIE). That was a wall the last time I was here and every other fecking time.

He takes in the room.

Are you going for the Scandi look or what?

BEIV. Just wanted a bit more light.

COLM. Think the neighbours can get enough of a look-in?

BEIV. I don't care.

COLM. At night when the lights are on, you'll see straight in from the road.

BEIV. So?

COLM. Well is that what you're going for?

BEIV. I've nothing to hide.

COLM. Jesus.

COLM *shakes his head.*

He walks around looking at things.

BONNIE. Everyone's bitter about their childhood. My mom is so neurotic, she like totally fucked us all up.

COLM *peers behind the beaded curtain.*

COLM. Jesus! What's going on here?

BEIV *looks up.*

Where's the kitchen? And the bedroom? And the back wall?

BEIV. Oh.

She takes a calm sip of tea.

I knocked them down.

COLM. You what?

BEIV. I'm building an extension.

COLM. An extension?

BEIV. What else am I going to do with the money from the house?

COLM *stares in*.

COLM. But where are you sleeping?

BEIV. That couch is a fold-up.

COLM. And where are *we* going to sleep?

BEIV. There's a couple of mattresses out in the shed.

COLM. Mattresses!

BEIV. We'll drag them in here. Be nice and cosy.

COLM *looks at her incredulous*.

COLM. And you didn't think to mention this in the email, did you not?

BEIV. There were a few things you didn't think to mention either.

She glances at BONNIE.

COLM.…I told you Bonnie was coming.

BEIV. You didn't tell me she was your wife.

BONNIE. Oh we didn't tell anyone. Our friends, most of my family – my parents were the only real witnesses.

BEIV. So Bonnie's parents got the nod?

COLM. Don't be like that, Beiv. You've got a thing about planes.

BONNIE *looks at* BEIV, *concerned*

BONNIE. Oh – did you want to come?

COLM. She wouldn't have.

BEIV. How do you know I wouldn't have?

COLM. Eleven hours to San Francisco, yeah right.

BEIV. I'd come if I'd a good reason. My son's wedding is a good reason.

BONNIE. I'm so sorry.

COLM (*to* BONNIE). Don't be. (*To* BEIV.) You don't come to things.

BEIV. What haven't I come to? I was at your graduation. Carol services. Parent–teacher nights.

COLM. Dad did those.

BEIV. Not all.

COLM. Never came to my rugby matches.

BEIV. Well I can't support that.

COLM. Why not?

BEIV. Football, now that's a good working-class sport.

COLM. Is that right? Shouldn't have raised me in fucking Sandymount then.

BEIV. Or GA. Wouldn't have minded GA.

BONNIE. He said you had a beautiful house.

COLM. Fucking gorgeous.

BONNIE. Right by the sea.

COLM. Five minutes' walk. Could see the whole of Dublin Bay. Joyce's *Ulysses*, all that jazz.

BEIV. Should have stayed if you were so bloody fond of it.

COLM. I would have come back to say goodbye.

BEIV. To a house? Come on.

COLM. My house. That I grew up in.

BEIV. Well if you'd told me it meant so much to you, maybe I wouldn't have sold it.

COLM. Shouldn't have had to tell you.

He looks back into the kitchen.

Anyway, where are we going to sleep, seriously?

BEIV. I told you.

COLM. This is our honeymoon. (*To* BONNIE.) I'm sorry,
Bonnie, I didn't know.

BONNIE. It's okay. It's Beiv's home. Is it okay if I call you Beiv?

BEIV. What else would you call me?

COLM. It was my da's place actually. And any normal person
would have mentioned it. Said great you're coming but I've
actually knocked down the kitchen, and the bedroom and the
walls are sort of open and anyone can walk in – so really
there's no room to have guests.

BEIV. I'm fine with the two of yous on the couch, me on the
floor.

COLM. Well I'm not. And Bonnie's not.

BONNIE. I don't mind.

BEIV. Well if it's that much trouble, the Crowleys still have the
B&B.

COLM. The Crowleys? Are they nice to you now then?

BEIV. The Crowleys were always nice.

COLM. Thought he was the one who talked to the *Examiner*
that time.

BEIV. Ah, years ago.

COLM. Stupid fucker.

BEIV. He was just excited at the prospect of his name in the
newspaper.

COLM. Said what he thought though, didn't he?

BEIV. Well Sheila's very nice. She makes great banana bread.
I buy two off her every week.

COLM. Doesn't mean she doesn't think you're a murderer.

BONNIE. Colm.

BEIV *looks at him, calm.*

BEIV. Why don't you head down to The Anchor then? They've always got a few rooms.

COLM. Actually that's not a bad call. (*To* BONNIE.) That's the pub. Only one on the island but good views. They've trad sessions on the weekends. You'll like that.

BEIV. Not real trad.

COLM. It's all the same, it's fiddles and shit, she'll love it.

BONNIE *smiles sympathetically at* BEIV.

BEIV. Well let me give you something towards it.

COLM. Money?

BONNIE. Oh no /

BEIV. It's not cheap this time of year.

BONNIE. We don't need money, do we, Colm?

COLM. No.

BEIV. I'd like to contribute.

COLM (*firm*). We're fine.

Beat.

Thanks.

BEIV. Doing alright then, are you?

COLM. Grand thanks.

BONNIE. One of these days he's gonna create his own app or write some great code and become like one of those Irish software billionaires we're always reading about.

COLM. Bit past that I think, Bonnie.

BONNIE. You've great ideas.

COLM. Very happy to be working for the man right now, thanks very much.

BEIV. And you've bought a place, he says?

BONNIE (*pleased*). Oh yeah. It's great.

COLM. Just a one-bed.

BEIV. It's not cheap in San Francisco that's what I hear.

BONNIE. Not at all.

COLM. Not cheap anywhere.

BONNIE. But it's really nice.

BEIV. Well you'll have your cut of the house.

COLM. The house?

BEIV. In Sandymount. I got a good price. Sold at the right time I think. (*To* BONNIE.) It's all gone mad again here. We never learn.

COLM. You're alright.

BEIV. What?

COLM. I don't need the money from the house.

BEIV. Don't be silly.

COLM. I don't.

   COLM *and* BEIV *look at one another – something.*

BEIV. Suit yourself.

   BEIV *looks at her watch.*

   You'd want to get down there if you want a room. Ferry comes in at four and there's always a few stragglers that get too pissed and have to stay over.

COLM. Right.

   He grabs his jacket, heads for the door.

   Who owns the place now?

BEIV. A Belgian guy, Antoine. And his wife.

COLM. Nice?

BEIV. They were yeah.

COLM. Were?

BEIV. Ah you know.

COLM. Right.

BEIV. No they're fine. They'll be nice to you.

COLM looks at her, uncertain.

COLM. Well we'll stroll down and see what they have.

BEIV nods.

Coming, Bonnie?

BONNIE. I'm gonna stay with Beiv.

BEIV (*taken aback*). Oh no, there's no –

COLM (*to* BONNIE). You sure?

BONNIE nods.

BONNIE. My legs are really heavy from the plane. I think I'm getting my oedema back.

BEIV. You don't have oedema.

BONNIE. Oh my god, these are so swollen. Look!

She gestures to her perfectly normal-looking legs.

COLM rolls his eyes.

COLM. Cool. Back in ten.

He glances back towards the curtain. Shakes his head at the mess.

Jesus.

He leaves.

BONNIE and BEIV sit looking at one another.

Awkward silence.

BEIV. I might have some banana bread out in the freezer.

BONNIE. You have a freezer?

BEIV. There's still a kitchen out there. There's just not much left of the back wall.

BONNIE *gets up and looks*.

BONNIE.…Don't you get nervous that someone could come in?

BEIV. It's only temporary.

BONNIE. But doesn't it get cold?

BEIV. Why I'm doing it in summer.

She looks at BONNIE.

Do you want me to have a look? It's nice toasted with a bit of butter.

BONNIE. I don't eat grains.

BEIV. Bananas aren't grains.

BONNIE. The flour. Really bad for your gut lining.

BEIV. Oh. My gut seems to love it…

BONNIE. I can't believe I'm in your house.

BEIV *looks at her, surprised*.

Sorry. I didn't mean to go all fangirl. I just – I was an art history major. In college.

BEIV. Oh.

BONNIE. I mean I dropped out before I – Colm probably told you.

BEIV. Doesn't tell me anything.

BONNIE. Well it's been kind of 'a thing'. With my family. But Colm's been so cool.

BEIV. Has he?

BONNIE. Really supportive.

Beat.

Anyway, I studied you.

BEIV. Me?

BONNIE. We had to pick a contemporary artist and do a presentation and Colm told me about you. My tutor had actually heard of you.

BEIV (*dry*). Ah.

BONNIE. I had like a huge advantage cos Colm has all these pictures of your work.

BEIV. Has he?

BONNIE. I love that giant sculpture of your tampon.

BEIV. Oh god.

BONNIE. Colm *hates* it. It like totally grosses him out. But I think it's extraordinary.

BEIV *shifts, uncomfortable*.

BEIV. Well looking back, it was probably a bit – reductive.

BONNIE. No, it's incredible.

BEIV. I was in a bit of a temper with some of my contemporaries at the time. You know, hanging their knickers on a wall, saying it's art.

BONNIE. What, like Tracey Emin?

BEIV. Yes. Well no. At least she did it first. Well almost first. She's a very skilled draughtswoman, you know.

BONNIE. Okay.

BEIV. It was just this idea of truth having to be the *actual* truth, you know. Without the beauty of symbolism.

BONNIE. But a sculpture is symbolic?

BEIV. True.

BONNIE. And art is about truth, isn't it?

BEIV (*jaded*). I spose.

BONNIE. That's what's so beautiful about artists. They put themselves out there.

BEIV. Hmmn.

BONNIE. You *really* put yourself out there.

BEIV. Well now I'm going back to blood oranges. Much easier. Let me see what I have in the back.

BEIV *gets up, and goes into the kitchen.*

We hear foostering. Pots and pans being lifted.

BONNIE *hovers, looking around.*

BONNIE....I thought those paintings you did after your – after Colm's – father's... death were really beautiful. All those colours, the greens, the blues, the greys...

BEIV *keeps moving around inside.*

Even the name of the exhibition. '*Guilt.*'

A sudden silence from the kitchen.

BONNIE *feels a bit alarmed.*

That was really brave. Considering.

BEIV *comes out of the kitchen, holding a bowl of strawberries.*

BEIV. I don't know what people who don't eat grain eat.

She proffers them to BONNIE.

Berries?

BONNIE. I love berries.

BEIV *hands her the bowl.* BONNIE *takes one, eats it.*

Are these local?

BEIV *shrugs.*

BEIV. Got them in the Lidl. In town.

BONNIE. That's on the mainland, right?

BEIV. Don't feel like you have to talk about my work all the time.

BONNIE. Oh, I like talking about your work –

BEIV. Well maybe don't talk about it is what I'm saying.

BONNIE *is little startled.*

I mean I'm flattered that you like it. That's very kind. But Colm doesn't.

BONNIE. That's not necessarily /

BEIV. So I think we should just cool it on that front for the time being. If that's okay?

Beat.

BONNIE....Okay.

BEIV. Great.

BEIV *sits down in a chair.*

BONNIE *sits cross-legged on the floor with her bowl of berries.*

She looks at BEIV.

BONNIE. I think he's very proud of you, you know, deep down.

BEIV. Very deep.

She looks at BONNIE.

So what are you doing with yourself then if you've dropped out of college?

BONNIE. Oh different things. Like right now I'm doing a foundation course.

BEIV. In art?

BONNIE. Psychology. I'm going to become a Jungian analyst.

BEIV *raises an eyebrow.*

BEIV. Don't you need to be a bit older for that?

BONNIE. Oh I will be. It takes years to train. I'll be at least twenty-eight.

BEIV *takes this in.*

BEIV. Right.

BONNIE. In fact there are some schools of psychology, you could be training for the rest of your life.

BEIV. That's convenient.

BONNIE. Have you ever been to a therapist?

BEIV. Once or twice.

BONNIE. Did it help?

BEIV *shrugs*.

BEIV. Felt like a bit of an eejit to be honest. Sittin' there going on about myself.

BONNIE. Maybe you just didn't find the right one.

BEIV. Maybe.

BONNIE. You're supposed to try a couple and see which one resonates.

BEIV. My son being good to you, is he?

BONNIE *looks up, surprised*.

BONNIE. Good to me?

BEIV. Treating you well. With kindness and tenderness and respect.

BONNIE. Oh yes. Yeah. He's amazing. I'm so lucky. He's paying for this course actually. I mean I'll pay him back. It's not like – sponging now we're married.

BEIV. Why do Americans marry so young?

BONNIE. Do we?

BEIV. I think so. I see all these kids coming over on the ferry. Twenty-five, twenty-six, with wedding bands and life plans. No one in their right mind should get married before thirty. Forty if they can help it. Any earlier should be illegal.

BONNIE *smiles*.

BONNIE. Why?

BEIV. You don't know yourself. Not to mention the person you're marrying – and they don't know themselves either for that matter...

BONNIE. I think I know myself pretty well.

BEIV. Course you do, you're twenty.

BONNIE. Three.

BEIV. Ah.

BONNIE. My parents got married young and they've been married for like twenty-five years so statistically I'm in a good position. If you come from an intact family you're more likely to have healthy attachment skills.

BEIV. That right?

BONNIE *nods*.

BONNIE. Although my dad's like a total enabler so…

BEIV *looks out the window*.

I'm really interested in the human psyche.

BEIV. Who isn't.

BONNIE. Some people aren't actually.

BEIV. They're just afraid of what's in there.

BONNIE. That's what I think.

BONNIE *glances up at the painting about to remark on it, but* BEIV *gets up suddenly*.

BEIV. I think I'll take a little walk down to the beach.

BONNIE. Beach?

BEIV. There's a little pebble beach about ten minutes from here. Always clears my head.

BONNIE. Can I come?

BEIV *hesitates*.

BEIV. Thought your oedema was at you.

BONNIE. It's okay. If you want to be on your own.

BEIV. No no.

BONNIE. I'm just really excited to be here.

BEIV. Well come, if you like.

BONNIE. You sure?

BEIV *nods*.

BEIV....Sure.

BONNIE. Great! I'll just get my shoes on.

> BONNIE *gets up excitedly, goes to where she's left her shoes by the door.*

> *As she pulls them on –*

It's weird cos I thought the jetlag would hit so much harder.

> BEIV *stares out the window. The faint sound of the sea.*

But actually I feel fine. I feel really really awake now.

BEIV. I'm glad he's being good to you, my son. That's important.

> BONNIE*'s slightly unsure how to respond.*

> *She stands up straight and smiles.*

BONNIE....Ready.

Two

The cottage is empty. BEIV *and* BONNIE *have gone.*

COLM *comes back to get the bags.*

He's looking around when suddenly the door opens and DONAL, *wearing overalls and carrying a sack of clay, enters. He sees* COLM *and stops.*

DONAL. Jesus fuck!

COLM (*seeing him*). Donal!

> DONAL *drops the clay –*

DONAL. How the hell are you, man?

> *Embraces* COLM.

COLM. Good, great. I didn't /

DONAL. She said you were coming down alright.

COLM. Did she, yeah?

COLM *takes an awkward step back*. DONAL *assesses him*.

DONAL. God. You look the exact same.

COLM. Do I?

DONAL. Except for…

He gestures to something on COLM*'s face – maybe a beard?*

COLM. Oh yeah. /

DONAL. Very hipster like.

COLM (*dry*). Thanks.

DONAL. No I like it.

COLM *flushes a bit*.

COLM. How's things with you anyway?

DONAL. Good. In pretty good form actually. Considering.

COLM. You're back.

DONAL. Few months ago, yeah. Did Beiv not tell you?

COLM. No.

DONAL*'s surprised*.

You were out in Australia, yeah?

DONAL. Australia. Bali. New Zealand for a bit.

COLM. Nice.

DONAL. New Zealand's beautiful. Like here but like waaay better.

COLM *laughs*.

COLM. I did a few months over in Sydney after college – wasn't really my bag.

DONAL. No I can imagine.

COLM. What does that mean?

DONAL. Just – you like your creature comforts. Slumming it in a room with five stinking lads, was never really your scene.

COLM. Bet you fucking loved it.

DONAL. Too right I did.

DONAL *grins*.

COLM *smiles*.

Jesus, look at you.

COLM. ...What?

DONAL *reaches out, touches* COLM*'s collar.*

DONAL. Bit smart for island life, isn't it?

COLM. What? / It's just a –

DONAL. Lacoste?

COLM. No.

DONAL. Ralph La– fuckin – Lauren.

COLM. Fuck off.

DONAL. Silicon Valley, darling.

COLM. She's been blabbing I spose?

DONAL. Course she has. Proud mam. Anyway, I'm the one doing the patio so I'm a sitting duck.

COLM (*surprised*). You're doing the patio?

DONAL *nods. Takes out some tobacco and rolling papers.*

DONAL. Thank god. Fuck-all else work round here. Except for the ferry, like.

He offers some to COLM*, who shakes his head.*

DONAL *opens the front door, as he rolls.*

COLM. So what happened with the bar and everything?

DONAL. Lost that in the break-up.

COLM. Oh. Sorry.

DONAL *shrugs*.

DONAL. My ex was Aussie, they move on quickly. Week after we finished he'd met someone else.

COLM. Harsh.

DONAL. And we know what I'm like so…

Brief beat.

Anyway in the end I just wanted out of there, so when he offered to buy my share I thought…

COLM. Why not?

DONAL. Exactly.

COLM. Least you got some money out of it.

DONAL. Spent it all travelling. Figured taking loads of drugs on a beach in Thailand would sort my broken heart.

COLM. Did it?

He looks at COLM, *tries to smile*.

DONAL. No.

DONAL *lights up*.

When was the last time you were even down here?

COLM. Ah years ago. Maybe just after Dad…

DONAL. No I've seen you since then.

COLM. The summer after?

DONAL. Yeah it was the summer after.

COLM. Nine years ago then.

DONAL. You flew back for that – I dunno what would you call it /

COLM. That's right. /

DONAL. Like a mind.

COLM. A remembrance, Beiv called it.

DONAL. That's it. A rememberance. For old Mike.

COLM. Jesus, we were bollixed.

DONAL. We were langers.

COLM. Beiv too.

DONAL. She was in bits. I mean your old lady can hold her booze but that night…

They laugh.

I've actually had some pretty big nights with her these past few.

COLM. Have you yeah?

DONAL. Ah yeah. Nice to have someone to shoot the shit with who actually has something to say.

COLM. Oh she's got plenty to say alright.

DONAL *smiles*.

Shit hadn't hit the fan yet back then o'course.

DONAL. No. Not at that stage.

COLM. Ignorance is bliss.

DONAL *glances at him*.

DONAL. She's doing good now, though.

COLM. Don't know what the fuck she's doing down here to be honest.

DONAL. She likes it, she says. She can work.

COLM. Yeah, but she can blend up in Dublin.

DONAL. Most of the locals'd be grand about her. It's the ones off the ferry you've to keep an eye on.

COLM. Well she's determined to give them a good enough look at her. With this.

He gestures to the window.

DONAL. You don't like it?

COLM. It's a bit exposed.

DONAL. Gonna be the same out the back.

COLM. What?

DONAL. Yeah she's gonna knock the kitchen into this room. Put a big glass patio out the back. Glass on all sides, bit of wall in between.

COLM. So what – she'll basically be living in a glass box?

DONAL. Think it'll be beautiful.

COLM. You're facilitating this?

DONAL. No, she's got some architect fella from Dublin drawing up the plans. She just – asks my opinion from time to time. Which I appreciate.

COLM. And you don't think it's a bit mad?

DONAL. It's her cottage.

COLM. No, it was Dad's cottage.

DONAL. And he was good to leave it to her.

COLM. Wasn't he just.

    DONAL *studies him*.

DONAL. They were always unusual, Colm.

    COLM *laughs, bitter*.

COLM. One way of putting it.

DONAL. Not many divorced couples you know still go on holidays together. But she was down here every summer with himself, well after you'd gone off to the States.

COLM. I know.

DONAL. How long have you been over there now?

COLM. Thirteen years this winter.

DONAL. You're never coming back.

COLM. If I can help it.

    A flicker from DONAL.

    He stubs out his cigarette

DONAL. Want a beer?

COLM.…Sure.

> DONAL *goes into the kitchen, comes back out with two cans of Foster's.*

> *They open the beers and drink throughout the following.*

How's your ma doing?

DONAL. Flying it, yeah. Delighted to have me back. Thinks she can bribe me with food, so's I won't leave again.

COLM. Well it's a beautiful place for the summer.

DONAL. And I don't plan on putting down another winter. Last one nearly killed me.

COLM. That's what I said to Beiv. It's one thing coming down here for a few weeks in July when the weather's nice and the Dublin crowd are out with their fecking yachts or whatever, but winter. That sky closing in…

DONAL. You were never here in winter.

COLM. Yeah I was.

DONAL. When?

COLM. First term of college.

> DONAL *smiles.*

DONAL. Oh right. When you ran away.

COLM (*quiet*). Yeah.

DONAL. We had this place to ourselves for a week till the old lad tracked you down.

> COLM *looks down, shy.*

COLM. It was pissing it down the whole time anyway.

DONAL. As I remember, we didn't spend too much time outside.

> *A beat.*

> COLM *looks away.*

COLM. What's she been up to anyway?

DONAL. Who?

COLM. Beiv.

DONAL. Nothing. Getting this place ready. Building a patio.

COLM. What's she building a patio for?

DONAL. She's allowed to have a patio.

COLM *shrugs, surly.*

She's distracting herself probably after all the recent hoo-ha – with this podcast.

COLM. What podcast?

DONAL. You don't know about the podcast?

COLM. No.

DONAL. Oh some fucking langer's doing a podcast.

COLM. Seriously?

DONAL. They're all at it now since that *Serial* one. Not enough murders to keep up with demand.

COLM. And he's been giving her hassle?

DONAL. No, no. Not him. Well could be him. Someone was calling here at all sorts, knocking on the door, writing shit on the walls.

COLM. What did they write?

DONAL. Just shit. I told her not to worry about it.

COLM. Someone local like?

DONAL. I dunno – we got the guards over but… you know how it is. Anyway, told her she can call me anytime and I'll be straight down. Day or night. Just say the word.

COLM *takes this in.*

COLM. Right.

DONAL *nods.*

COLM *looks at him.*

Thanks.

He shakes his head.

A podcast... that's all we fucking need.

DONAL. Ah sure I felt for her when I heard. Knew it'd a bring another whole heap o'shit, but she's strong, Beiv. She'll bear up.

COLM. She been seeing anyone?

DONAL. Ah now.

COLM. Just curious.

DONAL *shrugs.*

DONAL. There was a woman alright used to visit... From Wicklow.

COLM. Wicklow?

DONAL. Maybe. I don't know what the deal was. They could've been friends.

COLM. Beiv doesn't do friends. Pardon the...

COLM *takes a disapproving swig of his drink.* DONAL *smiles.*

DONAL. What's it to you anyway? Your mother's sex life. Bit Oedipal.

COLM. I'm just trying to figure her out.

DONAL. Beiv? Not possible. You know that.

COLM *takes a big drink, then crushes his can.*

He looks at the suitcases.

COLM. I should probably get going. Take these down to The Anchor.

DONAL. You're staying at The Anchor?

COLM. Well, we can't stay in this tip.

DONAL. We?

COLM *looks at him.*

COLM....just got married.

DONAL. No way!

DONAL *looks down at* COLM's *finger, clocks the ring.*

Shit, I didn't even see that. Congratulations, man.

COLM. Thanks.

DONAL. No seriously that's fucking – that's great news. Beiv
never said a word.

COLM. Well /

DONAL. We should have a drink.

COLM. Okay.

DONAL. Celebrate.

COLM. Cool.

DONAL. I'd love to meet him.

COLM....Her.

DONAL. Okay. Yeah.

DONAL *takes a swig of his drink.*

COLM. Bonnie. She's American.

DONAL. And lies over the ocean, does she?

COLM. No, she's here.

DONAL. Yeah, I – I know – (*Quickly.*) where's she from? In
America?

COLM. California.

DONAL. Cool. Well I'd love to meet her. Tonight or tomorrow
or –

COLM. We're around for ten days or so.

DONAL. Well whenever.

They look at one another. Something.

COLM. You'll like her. She's great.

DONAL. Course… she married you.

COLM *looks down awkward.*

COLM. Right so.

COLM *grabs the suitcases and heads for the door.*

DONAL. Hey. You know I was only messing with that Oedipal thing, don't you?

COLM. Course. He wanted to fuck his mother. Whereas I can barely fucking stand mine.

Beat.

Later.

DONAL. Yeah.

COLM *goes.*

DONAL *takes a swig of his beer, watches after him.*

Three

A table in the middle of the room – three or four skulls on it.

Mostly animal skulls but one replica of a human skull that looks startlingly real.

BEIV *stands at a smaller easel doing a charcoal sketch of them.*

BONNIE, *wet hair, wearing an oversized jumper over her swimsuit, is examining the human skull.*

BONNIE. It looks so real…

BEIV. Hmmnn.

BEIV *keeps sketching.*

BONNIE. It's not though, is it?

BEIV *gives her a look.*

Where did you get it?

BEIV. Internet. They supply them to medical students. I've got tibulas and fibulas somewhere there in a box.

BONNIE *turns the skull over in her hand.*

BONNIE. It's so – dirty and kind of weather-worn. Like it's been sitting in the earth for –

BEIV. Ten years?

BONNIE. Yeah.

BEIV. That's the idea.

BONNIE *glances at her, uncertain.*

BEIV *keeps sketching.*

BONNIE. So how do you do it?

BEIV. What?

BONNIE. Get that effect.

BEIV. Bit of paint, some earth, some turp. No particular technique.

BONNIE *puts the human skull down, picks up an animal skull.*

BONNIE. But these *are* real right?

BEIV *nods.*

BEIV. Got them from a farmer in Clon. He dug them up. No big deal to the guys round here. Animal bones are ten a penny.

BEIV *tries to see around* BONNIE.

BONNIE. Am I in your way?

BEIV. A bit.

BONNIE *steps back, quickly.*

BONNIE. Sorry.

BEIV. Where's Colm?

BONNIE. Out in the boat.

BEIV (*surprised*). Again?

BONNIE. Yeah.

BEIV. That's the third time in two days.

BONNIE. I know. I'd no idea he was such a great sailor.

BEIV. Got that from his dad.

BONNIE. Yesterday he took me round all the little islands. We stopped on one for lunch.

BEIV. Which one?

BONNIE. It had the name of an animal…

BEIV. Right.

BONNIE. Rabbit?

BEIV. Rabbit?

BONNIE. Anyway, it was beautiful. And Colm brought a picnic. Champagne, strawberries.

BEIV. Very romantic.

BONNIE. I won't get into what we did on the grass.

BEIV. Thanks.

BONNIE. I mean I know you're cool with all that. Not like my mom. She's from the Midwest. I've never even heard her say 'fuck'.

BEIV *keeps, sketching, concentrating.*

…Colm's so different at sea, don't you think?

BEIV. How do you mean?

BONNIE. Just more – commanding or in control or something.

BEIV. I suppose.

BONNIE. I like when he's like that.

BEIV. You didn't want to go out with him today?

BONNIE. Oh I did. But he asked me not to.

BEIV *looks up.*

BEIV. Oh.

BONNIE. Think he wanted some time to think. About his dad. He feels close to him on the water.

BEIV *goes back to sketching.*

BEIV. He used to be terrified of boats.

BONNIE. Colm? (*Disbelief.*) No!

BEIV. Absolutely petrified. Michael was very patient with him, actually. Cos every summer we'd have the same scene: life jackets on, coaxing him onto the boat, we'd finally get a few feet into the harbour and if there was even the smallest gust of wind, just the smallest bit, he'd grow completely hysterical. And we'd have to go back.

BONNIE. How did he get over it?

BEIV. Donal, I think.

BONNIE. Oh, right.

BEIV. You met Donal?

BONNIE. He came to The Anchor last night.

BEIV. He grew up here. Kids that grow up here, water's in their blood.

BONNIE. And Colm's dad grew up here too?

BEIV. Born and reared. He's the one who taught me to sail. Not that I go out much now but... he had that natural affinity with the sea.

BONNIE *nods.*

BONNIE. ...Until the last time I guess.

BEIV. Yes.

Silence.

BONNIE *feels strangely self-conscious.*

BONNIE. I love that big white monument up by the cliff. We passed it in the ferry.

BEIV. The beacon?

BONNIE. What is it?

BEIV. British ordered them all along the coast, supposedly, to alert ships to land.

BONNIE. It reminds me of an old seventies vibrator, or something.

BEIV *laughs*.

Is that offensive?

BEIV. Do I look offended?

BONNIE. I mean I think it's lovely, it's just the first thing I thought of.

BEIV. You can think anything you like. I'm not the tourist board. Probably why I've never made a sculpture of it.

BONNIE. Thought that would be a good reason *to* make a sculpture of it.

BEIV *smiles*.

BEIV. You're right.

BONNIE *looks back at the skulls. Trying to think of something to say.*

BONNIE. I really love what you're doing here.

BEIV. What am I doing?

BONNIE. Just… all this. Skulls.

BEIV (*dismissive*). Sure there's nothing original about skulls. Students learn on them. I'd have to encrust them with diamonds or something, but I think some other fella already thought of that.

BONNIE. But it's the context.

BEIV. Ah the context…

BONNIE. I just meant –

BEIV. I know what you meant.

BONNIE *looks at* BEIV*, aware she may have caused offence.*

But BEIV *keeps sketching.*

A beat.

How did Colm tell you about us?

BONNIE. How do you mean?

BEIV. How did he broach the subject of his family with you –
when you first met?

BONNIE. Oh…

BEIV. Did he just come straight out with it? Hi I'm Colm before
we get started I should probably let you know my mother –

BONNIE. No, no he didn't do that.

BEIV. Okay.

BEIV *keeps sketching, as* BONNIE *talks.*

BONNIE. Cos we met in a bar.

BEIV. Right.

BONNIE. Well after we met on our apps you know.

BEIV. Haven't a clue. But go on.

BONNIE. I think I would've been a bit freaked out if he'd just
come out with it. Cos it's pretty intense right?

BEIV. Right.

BONNIE. I mean he told me his dad was dead pretty quick, like
maybe our second or third date – and he said his mom was
a famous artist. Well kind of famous.

Beat.

In Ireland, you know?

BEIV. Uh-huh.

BEIV *keeps sketching, deadpan.*

BONNIE. But he didn't go into details or anything about –
Michael. He didn't tell me how or why or that they… you
know never found the – oh wow.

BEIV *looks up*.

BEIV. What?

BONNIE. Have you noticed how much death is a feature in your work?

BEIV....I have a pretty good idea.

BONNIE. Blood oranges, skulls...

BEIV. Yes.

BONNIE. That only just occurred to me.

BEIV. Carry on.

BONNIE. Hmmn?

BEIV. With what you were saying?

BONNIE. What was I saying?

BEIV. That Colm didn't tell you how Michael died until –

BONNIE. Oh. Right before the wedding.

BEIV *looks up, surprised*.

BEIV. Before the – you mean only a few weeks ago?

BONNIE. I guess. Yeah, I guess it *was* a few weeks ago.

BEIV. He only told you then?

BONNIE *nods*.

BONNIE. I mean I knew already, obviously. Cos I did that presentation and like, googled the shit out of you, so I kind of knew everything. I just – didn't say it to Colm.

BEIV. Why not?

BONNIE *shrugs*.

BONNIE. In case it was – intrusive or something. I didn't want him to hate me.

BEIV *is slightly impressed*.

BEIV....Weren't you shocked?

BONNIE. When I read it? A little. And I get why he wouldn't
have told me, I totally get that – but to tell you the truth…

She looks at BEIV.

…I think it's kinda great.

She corrects herself.

I don't mean the accusations or whatever. Obviously those
are – awful and sensationalised and ridiculous. I mean more
like the whole thing.

BEIV. What whole thing?

BONNIE. Like the fact you started like a women's commune.

BEIV (*embarrassed*). Oh Jesus. /

BONNIE. Here on the island. /

BEIV. It wasn't a commune. Where did you read that?

BONNIE. Just online.

BEIV. It was an artist's community. And it only lasted a couple
of months.

BONNIE. I know. I was so disappointed. I was hoping we'd
rock up here and there'd be like hundreds of naked women
lying on the grass reading – Yeats.

BEIV. Yeats?

BONNIE. Or something. (*Excited.*) I'd be really into that.

BEIV. I wouldn't.

BONNIE *stops*.

BEIV. And it wasn't hundreds – more like six or seven. Sorry to
ruin a good story.

BONNIE. How come it didn't work out?

BEIV. Cos I couldn't stand it.

BONNIE (*surprised*). The women?

BEIV. The whole thing. That they were here all the time. In my
space. I couldn't get any work done.

BONNIE. But… wasn't it sposed to be a community?

BEIV. Well, turns out I don't really like community.

BONNIE. Oh.

BEIV. Turns out community is a lot of work. And some of them were very needy. I don't do well with needy people.

BONNIE. I'm like totally the opposite.

BEIV. I've gathered.

Silence.

BONNIE. And – Michael just let you do it? Let you come here and start a community in his house with your – girlfriends?

BEIV. We were separating at the time. He was in Dublin. He was probably glad I was out of his hair. But yes, he let me do it.

BONNIE. That's amazing.

Beat.

You must have been very close

BEIV. Yes.

Beat.

BONNIE. And where was Colm when you were doing all this?

BEIV. Studying for his leaving cert.

BEIV *looks at her.*

I was a ferociously selfish mother.

BONNIE. Oh no I wasn't – judging.

BEIV. I don't deny it. And I certainly can't take it back now.

BONNIE*'s not sure what to say.*

BONNIE. Well, you can't have been that bad, cos he can't wait to have kids.

BEIV (*surprised*). Colm?

BONNIE. He talks about it all the time. I mean I'm not ready, *at all*. But it's nice that he says it, I think.

BEIV *goes back to her sketching.*

BONNIE *hovers a little awkwardly.*

So do you consider yourself gay or straight or –

BEIV. I consider myself lucky at the moment.

BONNIE. How do you mean?

BEIV. I've had relationships with men and I've had relationships with women. And all of them have been difficult in different ways. Eventually I had to accept the fact there was one common denominator to all these difficult relationships.

BONNIE. What?

BEIV *looks at her.*

BEIV. Me.

BONNIE. So… you're celibate?

BEIV. I think we've done enough talking for today.

BONNIE*'s taken aback.*

BONNIE. Oh sorry.

BEIV. I have a lot of work to do.

BONNIE. Sorry. Yeah – do you want me to go?

BEIV. I'm perfectly happy for you to join me.

BEIV *tears off a large scrap of paper, hands it to* BONNIE.

Here. Draw something.

BONNIE. Oh no, I'm really not much of an artist.

BEIV. Then yes I'd like you to go.

A startled beat.

BONNIE.…Okay.

BONNIE *turns.*

…sorry if I was distracting.

BEIV. Put your ego away, Bonnie.

BONNIE *looks at her, confused.*

BONNIE. Huh?

BEIV. This is not about me being rude or hurting your feelings or rejecting you, though if you choose to see it that way I won't stop you.

BONNIE *looks at her, uncertain.*

This is about me needing to do some work now because believe it or not this is what I do. This is a working day for me. And at the end of it I have to have something to show myself or I won't be able to live with myself – such is the life of an artist, so you can either take part in that or you can go outside and lie on the beach and enjoy your honeymoon. Either way, it's not personal and it's up to you.

BONNIE....Okay.

BEIV. Okay?

BONNIE *tentatively takes the sheet of paper.*

BONNIE. So –

BEIV. You just can't talk any more. Understand?

BONNIE. Sorry.

BONNIE *looks at the paper.*

I'm just a little embarrassed cos –

BEIV. I don't care what you draw.

BONNIE *stares at her.*

I won't be looking at it. I will be looking at my own work. That's how the work gets done.

She gestures to the table.

So now there's charcoal, there's pencils, there's paints on that table. Help yourself, use whatever you like. Just try to do it in silence.

BEIV *goes back to her sketching.*

BONNIE *tentatively goes to the table, picks up a piece of charcoal.*

She kneels on the floor and straightens her piece of paper.

She glances at BEIV, *uncertain.*

But BEIV *keeps working, not looking at her.*

BONNIE *tentatively starts to draw something.*

After a while –

I'd like to invite you and my son to have dinner tomorrow?

BONNIE....Oh.

BEIV. You've been here a few days, I haven't seen much of him. I think we should make a formal arrangement?

BONNIE. Okay. Sure.

BEIV. Will he come?

BONNIE. Course he'll come. He's here to see you.

BEIV. I'm not too sure about that. I'll invite Donal too.

BONNIE *seems a little less enthusiastic about that.*

BONNIE....Okay.

BEIV. We'll have a little party. Drown out any family intensity.

BONNIE. Sounds great. I'll tell him when he gets back.

BEIV *nods, starts sketching again.*

Hey. How do you get the charcoal to –

BEIV *puts her hand to her mouth, a gesture of silence.*

BONNIE *does an 'oops' gesture.*

Sorry. I forgot.

They continue sketching in silence.

Four

The light dims and we watch BEIV *clear the table of animal skulls.*

She replaces them with a tablecloth, plates, cutlery.

She lights some candles round the room.

Then she picks up the human skull, looking at it closely.

She opens the front door and puts the skull outside on the porch.

She comes back in and goes into the kitchen.

Five

Late that night.

Empty glasses and bottles of wine on the table.

Some music in the background perhaps, maybe on an old record player.

BEIV, COLM *and* BONNIE *sit round drinking and laughing as* DONAL *is in full flight.*

DONAL. I was there at the table with the bottle of champagne hidden – you know, where he couldn't see it.

BEIV (*prompting*). Your best suit…

DONAL. My best suit, which I'd just lashed on ten minutes before, my heart fucking pounding but I'm like 'come on Donal, keep it together.' Next thing he comes in the door and I can see he's a bit tipsy from the way he's moving, but I'm so fucking excited I don't care. So he takes off his jacket and comes over to the table right, and he looks at me with this really sort of intense look on his face…

BONNIE (*excited*). Oh my god.

DONAL. And then he takes my face in his two hands – which he has never done before in his life by the way, so I'm getting really fucking excited – and he leans in really close

and he says – hang on, lemme try and get the accent –
'Think I'm gonna hit' – ah fuck that's not it hang on –

COLM. Get to the end!

DONAL (*faux Australian*). 'Think I'm gonna hit the scratcher, babe.' That's it. That's what he said.

COLM. Think I'm gonna hit the scratcher?

BONNIE. What's a scratcher?

DONAL. Aussie for bed.

COLM. So he just went to bed?

BONNIE. No!

DONAL. He just went to bed.

BONNIE (*disbelief*). He didn't propose?

DONAL. He'd no fucking intention of proposing! He'd just signed the lease for the bar, that was the big news he'd wanted to tell me. But then he'd gone out and got so langered celebrating he forgot even to do that.

BONNIE. But what about your family on Skype?

DONAL. Well obviously when he went off, I had to slink over to the computer and tell them – 'sorry, folks, sorry, Ma, false alarm, no engagement tonight'…

COLM. Jesus /

BONNIE (*laughs*). Oh no.

DONAL. I mean it's funny now, but at the time like I was fucking devo.

BEIV. *You* should've proposed to him.

BONNIE. Yes!

DONAL. Ah now.

BEIV. Why not?

DONAL. A girl can dream, Beiv.

They laugh.

COLM. So you saw yourself as the girl in the relationship?

DONAL *stops*.

DONAL. No, it's just a figure of speech.

COLM. Is it?

DONAL. Yeah.

COLM. Okay.

COLM *takes a drink*.

Must be some truth in it though.

DONAL *looks at him, mild irritation*.

DONAL. Not really. We were both blokes, we were cool with that.

COLM. So why *didn't* you ask him?

DONAL. I dunno – it was just him that had to ask me.

COLM *frowns*.

COLM. Why?

BONNIE. It was the energy of the relationship.

DONAL. Yeah exactly.

COLM. The energy of the relationship? Fuck off.

BONNIE. It's true. There's masculine and feminine energy in all relationships, it's not about gender or whether someone's gay or straight or trans, it's about the characteristics of the person, how they are in the world.

COLM. Tell me my money isn't paying for this shit.

BONNIE *looks mildly embarrassed*.

BONNIE. It's *true*. In same-sex relationships, one person can embody the masculine, the other the feminine and in heterosexual relationships the masculine person can be the woman, the feminine the man.

DONAL. That's very fucking interesting.

COLM. It's new-age bullshit.

BEIV. I think Bonnie's on to something actually.

COLM. Course you do.

BEIV. I was definitely the masculine one in my marriage.

COLM. Just cos Dad let you push him around doesn't mean he didn't have balls.

BEIV. I didn't say he didn't have balls, just that his energy was more…

COLM. What?

BEIV. Like that.

> BEIV *makes a 'flowy' gesture with her hands*.

And mine was more. Like that.

> *She makes a 'direct' gesture.*

COLM. Ah here.

BONNIE. I think that's really honest.

> COLM *takes a disapproving drink.*

DONAL. So at this table I'd say *you* embody the masculine –

> *He points to* COLM.

COLM. Too right.

DONAL. Bonnie's the feminine… and it's a tie between me and Beiv.

BEIV. A tie!

DONAL. You're not the one who's been laying down concrete on that fecking patio!

> BEIV *laughs.*

COLM. Oh yeah this famous patio.

BEIV. What's famous about it?

COLM. Just wondering why you even need it.

BEIV. Cos the place needs a bit of updating.

COLM. Yeah, but why now?

BEIV. Cos I have the money now. Your dad wouldn't want it falling to wrack and ruin.

COLM. Well we don't really know what he'd want, do we?

COLM *takes another drink, watches her.*

DONAL. Well for what it's worth I think it's going to look beautiful. Beiv's bringing that artist's eye – it's really paying off.

BEIV. Thank you, love. (*To* BONNIE.) You know Donal studied architecture for a bit?

DONAL. Ah listen.

BONNIE. Did you?

BEIV. Very talented.

DONAL. Messed up my degree.

BONNIE. How?

DONAL *shrugs.*

DONAL. Ah, long story. Started in Cork, then left and went to Dublin, that didn't work out so… in the end I dropped out.

BONNIE. Oh.

DONAL. Like you, Bonnie. Drop-outs, the pair of us.

COLM. Bonnie's not a drop-out.

DONAL. Oh I didn't mean to –

BONNIE. It's okay. I am.

DONAL *looks at* COLM.

DONAL. So when are we going to hear the story about how you proposed?

COLM. Oh god.

BONNIE *laughs.*

DONAL. Did he mess it up?

BONNIE. No. It was perfect.

DONAL. Did he have the ring?

BONNIE. He did.

> BONNIE *holds out her hand*.

> DONAL *and* BEIV *admire the ring*.

BEIV/DONAL. Ooh /

BONNIE. Tiffany's.

DONAL. Very nice.

COLM (*embarrassed*). Come on.

BEIV. What? We just want to hear.

BONNIE. He got down on one knee and everything. (*To* COLM.) Tell them…

COLM. No.

DONAL. Why?

COLM. Cos it's none of your business. It's a private thing, between me and Bonnie. It's not for anyone else.

BEIV (*backing off*).…Alright.

> BONNIE *looks a bit embarrassed*.

DONAL. Guess we're back to patios.

BONNIE. Actually I've noticed there are some beautiful houses on this island.

DONAL. Cos of all the artists.

BONNIE. Really – there are a lot of artists here?

BEIV. One or two.

DONAL. And they all fucking hate each other.

BEIV. That's not true.

DONAL. Healthy sense of competition, is it.

BONNIE. I love that old place up by the beach.

DONAL. Which one?

BONNIE. With the huge overgrown garden and the swing.

BEIV. Nuala O'Neill's.

COLM. There you are, Bonnie, that's a banshee for you.

DONAL. What?

COLM. She was asking me about banshees earlier.

DONAL. Ah fuck. You weren't! I thought better of you, Bonnie.

BONNIE. I just didn't know what they were.

DONAL. Be leprechauns next.

COLM. Well Whiskers is as about close as you'd get.

BEIV. Don't call her Whiskers.

DONAL (*to* BONNIE). We called her Whiskers cos of the hairs
    that grew out of her face and the fact that she always bought
    a load of cat food.

COLM. And didn't have any cats.

DONAL. She'd feed the strays.

COLM. I reckon she was living on it.

BONNIE. No!

COLM. Didn't she flash us once?

DONAL. Oh Jesus.

    They laugh.

COLM. Out by the gate in her nightie.

    DONAL *covers his eyes.*

DONAL. Stop. I'm getting pictures now…

BEIV (*serious*). Poor woman.

COLM. Poor woman! She was probably a paedo.

BEIV. She wasn't a paedo. She was a tragic creature who lost
    her only son and was never right since.

COLM. So it's alright to go flashing kids then?

BEIV. Probably didn't know what she was doing. Poor thing.

COLM. What's poor about her? She has the biggest house on the island.

BONNIE. Where is she now?

BEIV. Dead.

COLM *stops, surprised.*

COLM. No! When?

BEIV. Couple of years ago. I wasn't here.

DONAL. Me neither.

COLM *seems a bit taken aback.*

COLM. …How did she go?

BEIV. In her own home. Fair play to her.

DONAL. Council's trying to claim the place now or something, but there's loads of legal shit. Cos she willed it to the son. The dead one.

BONNIE. How did he die?

BEIV. Drowned. As a young lad.

COLM. That's right.

DONAL. Didn't they reckon there was something wrong with him? Like he was a bit simple or something?

COLM. Was he?

DONAL. Think so. Think my old lad said something like that once. They were about the same age… he wasn't much for local gossip though so, hard to pump him for info.

BEIV. Place like this, people close ranks.

COLM. They haven't for you.

BEIV. I'm not one of them.

DONAL *puts his arm around her.*

DONAL. Ah, you are, Beiv.

BEIV. That's kind. But I'm not.

COLM. Dad was always good to Nuala anyway. Whenever we'd get down here in summer, he'd bring a load of shopping over and we'd drop it up to her house.

DONAL. Sounds like Mike alright.

BONNIE. Really? Was he kind?

DONAL. He really felt for other people.

BEIV. Too much, sometimes.

COLM. I fucking hated going up there. Place stank to high heaven of piss. Newspapers all over the floor. I remember one time Dad tried to clean it up a bit, you know wash her cups and stuff cos there was mould growing all over everything, but it got too much. Eventually he gave up. He was pretty cut up about it though. Seeing her in that state.

BONNIE. That's so sad.

DONAL. Shouldn't really have been up there on her own.

BEIV. People want to be near to their dead.

COLM. Is that what you're doing?

BONNIE. Colm…

COLM. Just asking.

DONAL *raises his glass.*

DONAL. Anyway, she's in a better place now, old Whiskers.

COLM. We hope.

They drink.

BEIV *starts to clear away some plates.*

BEIV. Have you had enough to eat, Bonnie?

BONNIE. Yes, thank you.

BEIV. You were able to eat around the grains?

BONNIE. Can I help?

BEIV. Stay where you are. I've made it my life's mission not to be cleaning up after people, especially men, but on this one occasion I'll make an exception. Sit down, sit down. (*To* DONAL.) Put on some music.

DONAL *gets up and goes to the player.*

BONNIE. Wow. There's a lot of dark history here.

COLM. No wonder they're making podcasts.

DONAL. Let's talk about something more uplifting, will we?

COLM *ignores him.*

COLM. Have you heard about this podcast, Beiv?

BEIV. I have.

DONAL *puts on some music, low. Fleetwood Mac's 'Dreams'.*

BEIV *takes the plates into the kitchen.*

COLM. What do you think about it?

BEIV. Not much.

COLM (*calling*). So you're not worried then?

BEIV (*from inside*). About what?

BONNIE. Oh I love this song.

DONAL *comes back to the table.*

DONAL. Me too.

BONNIE *starts singing the first line of 'Dreams'.*

Nice voice.

BONNIE. Thank you.

BEIV *comes back in.*

COLM. You're really not worried about what people are going to say?

BEIV *looks at* COLM.

BONNIE *keeps singing*.

Can you stop that for a second?

BONNIE *stops singing*.

BONNIE. Colm…

COLM. What?

BONNIE. You're being a little obnoxious.

COLM. So are you. But you're American so you don't notice.

BONNIE *sits back, wounded*.

Can I turn this down?

BEIV. I'll do it.

BEIV *goes over to turn down the music*.

COLM *reaches over and pours himself a large glass of red wine*.

DONAL. Beiv says you've been out in the boat a bit.

COLM. Yeah, well we've had the weather so.

BONNIE (*to* DONAL). Actually she said you got him over his fear.

COLM *looks up sharp*.

COLM. What fear?

BONNIE. Of boats.

COLM. What? Fuck off.

BONNIE. When you were a kid. It's not an affront to your masculinity.

DONAL. In fairness you did used to piss yourself.

COLM. Why are you saying this shit?

DONAL. Cos it's true.

BEIV *comes back out*.

BEIV. My point was that you conquered your fear.

BONNIE. Exactly. You're great on the water.

COLM (*to* BONNIE). Oh and you'd know all about it, would you. With all your expertise.

BONNIE *frowns*.

DONAL. Well I don't think I can take credit for getting him out on the water. More like it was those fancy sailing lessons his dad bought him. Big thing in the summers here. All the posh kids from the cities come down and kick us yokels out of the sea. That right, Colm?

COLM. Not how I remember it.

DONAL. Spose you weren't the worst of them.

COLM. Thanks.

DONAL *smiles at* COLM, *good-natured*. COLM *shrugs, petulant*.

BEIV. Who's having ice cream? I got three flavours.

COLM. No thanks.

He takes a slug of wine.

BEIV....Bonnie?

BONNIE. Maybe later.

BONNIE *looks at* COLM.

You're drinking a lot tonight.

COLM. Well. When in Rome –

DONAL (*to* BONNIE). And he's the one complaining about stereotypes.

DONAL *gets up from the table*.

I'm going for a quick smoke.

BEIV. Will you roll me one?

DONAL. Thought you quit.

BEIV. Social occasion. Doesn't count.

DONAL. Anyone else?

> BONNIE *shakes her head.*

BEIV. Back in a sec. Help yourself to the ice cream –
(*To* BONNIE.) there's berries in the fridge.

BONNIE (*polite*). Thanks.

> *They go.*

> COLM *and* BONNIE *are left alone.*

> *Silence.*

> COLM *takes a swig of his wine, looks at her.*

COLM.... What's wrong with you?

BONNIE. Me?

COLM. Why are you being like this?

BONNIE. *You're* the one being rude.

COLM. She doesn't care.

BONNIE. You're being rude to *me.*

COLM. Cos you don't see what she's doing.

BONNIE. What is she doing?

COLM. Fucking with you.

BONNIE. By making us dinner?

COLM. You don't get it.

> *He sits back.*

BONNIE. No, I don't – get it.

COLM. Cos you're too busy sucking up to her.

BONNIE. Excuse me?

COLM. You're gonna deny it? 'Tell me about your art, Beiv,
tell me about banshees, Beiv, and faux-lesbianism and the
rest of your hippy-ass bullshit.'

BONNIE. I'm *interested*.

COLM. Is that all it is? Cos you couldn't have your head any further up her ass.

BONNIE. Oh my god, you so need therapy.

COLM. And will you shut up about therapy for five minutes. Jesus, sometimes I'm so fucking embarrassed listening to you –

BONNIE. Oh really?

COLM. All this crap about energy and femininity and 'oh your accent is so cute' /

BONNIE. I never said anyone's accent was / cute –

COLM (*over her*). Like everything every eejit here says to you is some sort of fucking poetic prophecy by dint of them just being fucking Irish. Do you know how we hate that here? Do you know what a cliché that is?

BONNIE gets up.

BONNIE. You're drunk.

COLM. Well I'd need to be, wouldn't I.

She looks at him, on the verge of tears.

BONNIE. You're also an asshole.

COLM. Where are you going?

BONNIE. Out.

She pushes past him. He grabs her arm.

COLM. Sit down.

BONNIE. Let go of me.

She tries to pull away – but he keeps holding on.

COLM. You were the one who wanted to come here.

BONNIE. To meet your family. Is that so terrible?

COLM. You don't know her like I do, alright.

BONNIE. I like her.

COLM. Well *don't* like her!

She tries to push past him again.

BONNIE. Will you please let me go.

COLM. Stop being such a fucking stupid little –

BONNIE (*fearful*). Stop it /

COLM. For fuck's sake /

BONNIE. TAKE YOUR FUCKING HANDS OFF ME RIGHT NOW, COLM.

COLM suddenly lets go.

He takes a shocked step back. BONNIE *turns on him, furious.*

Who the fuck do you think you are?

COLM puts a hand to his head, suddenly realising how drunk he is.

COLM. …I'm sorry. Bonnie, I'm sorry.

He comes towards her. She rushes to the door.

BONNIE. Stay the fuck away from me.

COLM. Bonnie…

She slams the door.

Bonnie!

She's gone.

COLM sways unsteadily. Staggers back to the table.

He picks up his glass of wine.

BEIV *comes into the room quietly. She looks at him.*

A beat.

Spose you heard all of that, did you?

BEIV. There's no walls here.

COLM. Very fucking convenient.

BEIV.... You don't think you should go after her?

He shakes his head.

COLM. She doesn't want me going after her.

He reaches for more wine.

BEIV *watches him, disapproving.*

What?

He fills his glass up, despite her.

BEIV. She's young, Colm.

COLM. So?

BEIV. So don't take your anger out on her.

COLM. Who says I'm angry?

BEIV gives him a look.

And if I am, maybe I have good reason.

BEIV. I'm not saying you don't have good reason, I'm just saying don't take it out on the girl.

COLM. What the fuck are you doing down here, Beiv?

BEIV. I told you –

COLM. No really. Why now?

BEIV. Why not?

COLM. Are they looking at the case again, or something?

BEIV looks down.

BEIV. They've just been talking about it.

COLM looks at her.

COLM. And you didn't think to tell me that?

BEIV. You know what it's like, every few years, there's some new – angle. It's just rumour.

COLM. I would *never* have brought Bonnie here –

BEIV. What is there to be concerned about?

COLM. Oh I don't know – maybe just the fact you were the
only person here the night he went out. Maybe just the fact
he'd changed his fucking will the week before so's
everything was tied up nice and neat to go to you.

BEIV. And you.

COLM. Maybe just the fact that none of this makes any sense.
He was an excellent sailor. It wasn't even that rough, why
didn't they find the body?

BEIV. It's useless going over and over this, Colm.

COLM. We haven't gone over and over it.

BEIV. Am I not entitled to be here if I want to be?

COLM. Does this sell your paintings or something, is that what
it is?

BEIV. Don't be facetious.

COLM. No I'm serious. It's obviously helped your reputation.

BEIV. That people think I killed my ex-husband?

COLM. It's a great publicity spiel.

BEIV. I'd like to think they like my work.

COLM. What – red blobs on a canvas?

BEIV. That's what you see.

COLM. That's what it is.

BEIV. You think I like this? People staring at me every time
I get on the ferry. Watching me in the street. Never sure if
someone's going to say hello or spit at me.

COLM. No one spits at you.

BEIV. You think?

COLM. Who spat at you?

BEIV. You think I like having them knocking at my door in the
middle of the night, writing things on the wall /

COLM. Then why come down here? No one did that shit in Dublin, no one gave a shit about you at all in Dublin.

BEIV. This is where I want to be.

COLM. Why?

Beat.

BEIV. It's my business.

COLM *stares at her.*

COLM. And that is what I cannot stand about you, Beiv. You're such a fucking hypocrite.

DONAL *appears awkwardly from the shadows*

DONAL....I'm... gonna head away I think, lads.

COLM. You've been lurking too?

DONAL. I was giving ye some space.

COLM. Last thing either of us needs is space, thanks.

BEIV. I'm going to get this place cleaned up.

DONAL. Want a hand?

BEIV. No thanks. I brought this on myself.

DONAL. Right...

DONAL *leans down to give* BEIV *a kiss on the cheek.*

Well I'll see you in the morning.

COLM *looks away, mild disgust.*

DONAL *goes to the door, looks back at* COLM.

You gonna be round tomorrow or...

BEIV. He'll head out with you now.

COLM *looks at her.*

COLM. Oh will I? Is that my cue to go?

BEIV. You're welcome to stay and tear strips off me but I don't think it'll do either of us any good.

COLM. Might do me some good.

BEIV. You're not going to get what you're after.

COLM. And what am I after?

BEIV. Blood. I think.

COLM. Jesus. Always with the melodrama.

BEIV. I'm not the one being melodramatic. I was actually the one trying to make things right, believe it or not, Colm.

COLM. Thank you for the dinner. It was delicious.

COLM *picks up his half-full wine glass and drains it.*

He slams it back on the table, turns for the door.

He stops.

You know what I think?

He turns and looks at BEIV.

I think you're a liar. I've just never had the guts to say it to your face.

BEIV. Well now you have.

Silence.

COLM *turns and walks out.*

DONAL *stands awkwardly looking at* BEIV.

DONAL. Are you alright?

BEIV. Course I'm alright.

She starts to collect more dishes.

DONAL (*re: the dishes*). Why don't you leave those till the morning?

BEIV. Cos I can't stand dirty dishes in the sink, it's one of my things.

DONAL. If you need anything… I have my phone.

BEIV. I'll be grand.

DONAL *heads for the door.*

He hasn't changed much, has he?

DONAL *looks at her.*

DONAL. No. Not at all.

BEIV. Never should have sent him to a private school.

DONAL. He doesn't mean it, Beiv.

Beat.

BEIV. Go on. I'll finish up.

DONAL *goes.*

BEIV *continues gathering up plates.*

She brings them into the kitchen.

Dumps them down.

Then she comes back in and starts blowing out the candles on the table.

She stops, suddenly overcome with emotion and walks over to the couch.

She sits down and looks out the window.

The faint sound of the sea.

She takes a breath, trying to steady herself.

Suddenly the sound of something outside.

BEIV *looks up.*

A beat.

She gets up and walks to the door.

Another noise.

BEIV *opens the door, tentatively.*

…Donal?

Beat.

She steps out and looks around.

Donal?

Nothing.

She comes back into the room, closes the door.

A beat.

She pulls out the couch-bed, brushing down the blankets, etc.

Then she goes and turns off the rest of the lights, leaving only one lamp on by the couch.

BEIV *lies down, fully clothed, on the couch-bed and exhales heavily.*

Then she reaches over and turns off the one remaining lamp.

Darkness.

The sound of the sea.

The sound of BEIV *breathing.*

It goes on for a few seconds, rhythmical, calming.

Suddenly a loud bang at the window.

The sound of shattering glass.

End of Act One.

ACT TWO

Scene Six

BEIV *'s cottage. Evening, the next day*

A large crack now runs through the middle of the window where something was thrown at it.

COLM *is sitting on the couch, head in his hands; he looks edgy, exhausted.*

He looks around at BEIV *'s paintings and sculptures, maybe he sees the animal skulls or the tibias.*

DONAL *comes in.*

COLM *stands.*

COLM. Any sign?

> DONAL *shakes his head.*

DONAL. I spoke to Dinny, he says she definitely hasn't been on the ferry today and Tom says she didn't get on the last one last night either.

COLM. Is he sure?

DONAL. Says he is. Says there were only a few on it, mostly lads. He would've remembered her.

COLM. …Fuck.

> COLM *thinks.*

DONAL. Are you sure she didn't go back to The Anchor?

COLM. No. The bed was all made when I got in.

DONAL. And there's no way she could've come in and kipped for a couple of hours?

COLM. And made the bed?

DONAL. Well, made it herself like.

COLM. No.

DONAL. You're sure?

COLM. She wouldn't do that, she's messy.

DONAL. Maybe she got another room.

COLM. I asked them that. She didn't.

DONAL. Okay.

COLM *looks at him, panicked*.

COLM. What are we going to do?

DONAL *looks around*.

DONAL.... Where's Beiv?

COLM. Nuala O'Neill's.

DONAL. Nuala's?

COLM. She thinks Bonnie might have gone up there after all the – talk last night, you know.

DONAL. Oh right. Spose the place *is* empty. Be easy enough to break in.

COLM. What would she want to break in there for?

DONAL. She's the curious type.

COLM. Why do you say that?

DONAL. It's how she comes across.

COLM. You don't know her.

DONAL. I know.

COLM. You don't know what the fuck you're talking about.

DONAL. Take it easy.

COLM. How can I take it easy when this is happening?

COLM *paces*.

And don't think I'm not holding you accountable by the way.

DONAL (*surprised*). Me? Hang on – what have I got to do with it?

COLM. You know very well what you've got to do with it.

DONAL. What the fuck… are you serious?

COLM. Yes.

DONAL stares at him.

DONAL. You're honestly blaming me for –

COLM pushes him slightly.

COLM. Yes I'm blaming you!

DONAL pushes him back harder.

DONAL. Fuck you. You need to get a fucking grip.

The door opens and BEIV *comes in, stopping whatever was about to kick off.*

BEIV. Right.

The boys quickly move away from each other.

She looks at them, sensing the tension.

…She's not up there.

COLM. Well I could've told you that.

BEIV. Went up to the castle as well. Just in case… so she's not at the beaches, she's not at The Anchor.

DONAL. She didn't get the ferry back. Last night or this morning.

BEIV. They're sure?

DONAL. I've checked with everyone.

BEIV. And she left her phone in your room?

COLM. She didn't take it to dinner last night. It was still there this morning.

BEIV. Okay…

COLM starts pacing, panicked.

COLM. This is unbelievable. It's a tiny island – how could she have just –

BEIV. She wouldn't have got in a boat, would she?

COLM. What boat?

BEIV. There's plenty tied up by the pier.

COLM. She's not just going to get in any old boat.

BEIV. She'd had a few drinks. People think they can do all sorts in that state.

COLM. You actually think she'd go out in a boat? By herself.

BEIV. I don't know.

COLM. She can't sail.

BEIV. I'm not trying to scare you.

COLM. Well you *are*. You're scaring the shit out of me.

DONAL. We could call the Lifeboat.

BEIV. Give it another hour.

COLM. Well what if she *is* out there, another hour it'll be getting dark?

BEIV. She's not, don't mind me.

COLM *runs his hands through his hair.*

DONAL. What about the police?

BEIV *glances at him.*

COLM. Oh the police. Yeah, they're gonna fucking love this. Jesus I mean for one person in a family to go missing at sea, that's pretty... but *two*.

DONAL. No one said she's missing at sea.

COLM (*to* BEIV). I mean that's them locking you up and throwing away the key, isn't it?

DONAL. Stop it.

COLM. I'm just saying what we're all thinking.

DONAL (*a warning*). And I'm saying shut the fuck up, Colm. This isn't the time.

Both COLM *and* BEIV *look at him, surprised.*

We need to stay calm.

BEIV. There's no point bringing the police into this until she's gone twenty-four hours.

COLM. She almost has been.

DONAL. Have we looked everywhere?

COLM. Yes.

BEIV. And the last place we saw her was –

COLM. Here. You know it was here.

BEIV. Over dinner. Where she left upset after a row with you.

He looks up.

COLM. ...She wasn't that upset.

BEIV. She was.

COLM. We have fights sometimes. That's normal.

BEIV. She told you to take your fucking hands off her.

COLM *looks at her.*

COLM. Why are you saying this?

BEIV. Because they'll ask. You're the spouse, you're the first person they'll want to speak to and you'll have to tell them the truth.

COLM. And I *will* tell them the truth. I haven't done anything wrong.

BEIV *looks at him.*

BEIV. ...I know.

COLM. So why are you looking at me, like you think I have?

BEIV. I'm just suggesting we don't get the police involved until we know there's something to be involved in.

COLM. And how will we know that? When her corpse floats by?

DONAL. Stop it, Colm.

BEIV. What time did you get in at?

A flicker from COLM.

COLM....I dunno. Wasn't wearing a watch.

BEIV. They'll ask you. You left here around eleven. A couple of minutes later there was a rock thrown through my kitchen window and another there –

She points to the glass.

COLM. That was nothing to do with me.

DONAL. Might be to do with Bonnie though.

COLM. You think Bonnie threw a rock at the window?

DONAL. No, but like maybe the person who took her –

COLM. What – hang on, we think someone took her now?

DONAL. No but like – there have been a few weirdos hanging round.

COLM. Jesus Christ, you're doing my head in.

BEIV. Okay alright –

COLM. Why are you saying these things?

BEIV. Look we'll stop the speculating. It's doing us no good. She's probably asleep in some field somewhere, somewhere we haven't thought to look –

COLM. I can't take this. I can't... I need some air.

COLM *opens the front door and goes out.*

BEIV *and* DONAL *are left alone.*

BEIV. He should eat something.

DONAL. Do you want me to cook?

BEIV. There's no food. I was supposed to go across on the ferry, do a shop, but with all the shenanigans with the windows and this... the day got away from me...

She sits down, a bit weary.

DONAL. ...Sorry I – missed your calls last night. Must've had my phone on silent.

BEIV *studies him.*

BEIV. I ended up knocking into the Crowleys.

DONAL. Were they alright?

BEIV. Oh yeah, lovely. Sheila took me in for a cuppa, fed me banana bread. Seamus came down here with a baseball bat in case whoever it was, was still lurking.

DONAL. And they weren't?

BEIV. Nah. Long gone.

DONAL. I'm sure he was glad to have a snoop round the place anyway.

BEIV. He's not the worst of them, Seamus.

DONAL. I'd be careful. He's a talker.

BEIV. ...He doesn't know anything.

DONAL *glances at her.*

They wanted me to call the cops o'course. But after everything today, I'm very glad we didn't.

DONAL. We might still have to.

BEIV. Rather we kept them out of it for now.

DONAL. But if she doesn't turn up –

BEIV. What's it got to do with us? We barely know the girl.

DONAL *frowns.*

DONAL. She's Colm's wife.

BEIV. And she's clearly a bit...

DONAL. What?

BEIV. Unsteady. All that dropping in and out of college. Marrying a man she hardly knows...

DONAL. Does she hardly know him?

BEIV. She's flaky.

DONAL. Ah now.

BEIV. Trust me. I know flaky when I see it. I've seen my share.

> DONAL *takes this in.*

> *Beat.*

> …You didn't say anything, did you? To – Colm?

> DONAL *looks at her.*

DONAL.…No. No, course not.

BEIV. Good.

> *Long beat.*

DONAL.…I don't feel right about it though.

BEIV. You don't have to feel right about it.

DONAL. He'll find out eventually.

BEIV. Only if one of us tells him.

> *A crease of worry crosses* DONAL*'s brow.*

> *He drops it.*

DONAL. If tomorrow comes and Bonnie still hasn't turned up…

BEIV. Then we'll reassess.

> *Beat.*

> But if she *has* gone and done something stupid. I don't see why we all should be dragged into it.

> COLM *comes in holding the 'human' skull in his hand.*

COLM. What is this?

> BEIV *looks up, calm.*

BEIV. It's a fake skull.

COLM. Why's it sitting outside the front door?

BEIV. Cos I put it there.

He looks at her, incredulous.

COLM. Why?

BEIV. For a joke, I spose.

COLM. A joke.

BEIV. We know why people come up here.

COLM. You want them to think this is Dad?

BEIV. No.

COLM. You don't?

BEIV. You're being far too literal.

COLM. Oh you meant it metaphorically, did you.

BEIV. I don't know what I meant. I just put it there, thought people could take from it that what they will.

COLM. And what did you want them to take from it?

BEIV. Come on, Colm /

COLM. You're actually goading people.

BEIV. It was a joke! For all the ghouls who come up here to have something to look at. That's what they want, something to look at – I'm just giving it to them.

COLM. You want them to think you're guilty?

BEIV. A guilty person wouldn't do that.

COLM. Oh no? O.J. Simpson wrote a book called *If I Did It*.

BEIV. Okay I'm sorry. I'm sorry for trying to have a fucking sense of humour –

   DONAL *stands up, trying to defuse the situation.*

DONAL. Hey, hey. You know what… I think we're all pretty strung out here and we should – we should probably get some food or something.

   BEIV *and* COLM *look at one another.*

They do takeaway at The Anchor. I can go down, get us some chips, pizza, whatever you want...

BEIV. I wouldn't mind some chips.

DONAL. Done. Colm?

COLM. Can you get takeaway booze in The Anchor?

BEIV. I'd go easy on the booze tonight.

COLM. I'm a grown man, thanks very much.

DONAL. What do you want?

COLM *pulls out his wallet, takes out some money.*

COLM. Six cans of Foster's, two bottles of red.

DONAL *takes the money.*

DONAL....What kind of red?

COLM. I don't know. Shiraz? I don't fucking care.

DONAL. And to eat?

COLM. Anything.

DONAL. Okay so. Chips, Shiraz and... anything.

BEIV. Thank you, Donal.

DONAL. No bother...

DONAL *and* COLM *lock eyes for a beat.*

Then DONAL *goes out.*

COLM *sits back down. A long silence.*

COLM....Do you think I should call Bonnie's parents?

BEIV. What for?

COLM. Maybe she's phoned them.

BEIV. And maybe she hasn't. And wouldn't you be putting the fear of god into them if she hasn't?

COLM *suddenly crumbles a bit.*

COLM. Oh Jesus... I don't believe this is happening...

BEIV looks at him, surprised at this emotion.

I've never spoken to her like that before, you know. I've always treated her like – like a princess. And then I come here and within a few days, I'm this fucking monster... this fucking place... I don't know why I came back here.

He starts to cry.

A beat.

BEIV reaches over to console him.

He moves away, sharp.

She retreats.

BEIV. In my experience most women don't want to be treated like princesses anyway.

COLM looks up.

COLM. What?

BEIV. Princesses are powerless, anodyne creatures.

COLM. That wasn't my point.

BEIV. What do you want with a girl so young, Colm?

COLM. Why do you keep going on about that? She's an adult.

BEIV. She's not up to you. There's no challenge.

COLM. I don't want a fucking challenge.

BEIV. Men who go out with younger women like to be in control.

COLM. Is that right? Well she walked out of here last night of her own free will so I think that pretty much debunks that theory. And who are you to talk anyway, you're the most controlling fucking person I've ever met.

BEIV. I don't argue with that.

Beat.

It's just I looked at that girl the other day and I saw her whole future.

COLM *looks up, surprised.*

She's looking for a beacon. Someone to rescue her from the dark ocean of her life and give it some shape, cos she doesn't know what to make of it, god love her. And here you are, handsome software engineer, money, rings from Tiffany's, trips to Ireland. It's all like a fairytale now. But one day… she'll wake up and hate you.

COLM *stares at her, stunned.*

COLM. I lost my temper *once*.

BEIV. She'll hate you for giving her everything. For taking away her chance to do it for herself.

COLM. Is that what happened with you and Dad?

BEIV *frowns.*

BEIV. I did things for myself.

COLM. Yeah but he supported you. If he wasn't the big solicitor raking in the dough, you couldn't have been faffing around making – fannies out of clay or whatever. Could you?

BEIV. I do admire how you always come back to your central thesis.

COLM. Well artists love to sneer at commerce. At people like me, making money, as if that's some kind of sleazy occupation, but they need us, artists. Cos who else is going to buy their shitty art?

BEIV *looks at him.*

BEIV. He did support me, your father.

COLM. Exactly.

BEIV. Because he believed in me. And he trusted me, totally. The responsibility of the artist is to go to those places people don't want to go to – no matter how brutal, or uncomfortable or exposing – and he let me. He *never* tried to rein me in… and he knew that I was grateful.

COLM. How? Cos the way I see it you just sort of fucked him over.

BEIV. Yes, I fell out of love with him sexually –

COLM. Ah Jesus. /

BEIV. He found that hard to take. What man wouldn't?

COLM. Well I remember the screaming, I remember the rows.

BEIV. And they were terrible. But he did forgive me.

COLM. No, he was just too nice to tell you the truth.

BEIV. Which is what?

COLM. That he would've been better off with you out of his life. Running off to – women's communes and then running back when it didn't work out. He tried seeing other women, never lasted.

BEIV. Which is a shame. I would have liked him to have met someone else.

COLM. How could he? They were all too intimidated by the fact you'd show up here every summer, the big celebrated artist, and he'd drop everything to follow you around.

BEIV. Your father had his own struggles.

COLM. No he was fine before you left. And you should have just left. Properly. Instead of hanging around. You ruined his chance of happiness and now you're trying to ruin mine by telling me my wife hates me...

He turns away suddenly.

Jesus... I've a pain in my stomach from all this...

He leans against the window, looks out.

BEIV *watches him.*

...I wish he was here now. He wouldn't just be sitting round waiting for – god knows what. He'd have the lads out with their boats, he'd be looking for her. He'd be doing something.

BEIV. I hope so.

COLM. I know so. I know what he was like.

He thinks.

...I'm going out there.

BEIV *looks up, surprised.*

BEIV. Where?

COLM. In the boat. I'm going to look for Bonnie.

BEIV. It'll be dark soon.

COLM. I don't care. I'm not leaving her out there by herself.

BEIV. We don't even know that she is out there.

He starts to put on his jacket, determined.

Check the weather before you go.

COLM. It'll be fine.

BEIV. You don't know that.

COLM. I don't care what happens to me. I just want to find Bonnie. And if I don't find her tonight, first thing tomorrow we're getting the police.

BEIV. Okay.

COLM. No arguments.

BEIV. I'm not arguing.

COLM. We're getting them.

She nods.

BEIV. Okay.

Beat.

I'm just glad that at least you have an alibi.

COLM *looks at her, sharp.*

BEIV *holds his gaze.*

Then he turns around and walks out.

BEIV *pulls her cardigan around herself and goes to the window.*

The sound of the sea.

Seven

Shafts of very early-morning light come through the window.

DONAL *is asleep on the armchair. There is no one else there.*

The sound of footsteps, the door opens and COLM, *enters, exhausted.*

DONAL *wakes up.*

DONAL. Hey.

COLM....Hi.

COLM *takes off his jacket. Kicks off his boots.*

DONAL. You were out there all night.

COLM. Yep.

DONAL....We were worried.

COLM *goes into the kitchen, comes back with a can of beer.*

COLM. Where's Beiv?

DONAL, *still sleepy, looks at the empty sofa across from him.*

DONAL. She was there.

COLM. Done one of her disappearing acts, has she?

DONAL. She's probably gone looking for you.

COLM. Well I didn't see her.

COLM *sits down and opens the can.*

DONAL. Where did you go?

COLM. All over the place. Around the harbour, round all the islands, out to sea. Very tempting to just keep on going, sail right on over to America...

DONAL....And no sign?

Beat.

COLM....No.

COLM *takes a drink.*

It's weird, you know, cos it's a full moon. And the light on the water was so beautiful. Like a huge torch or something – just dancing all over the waves… You'd almost forget why you were out there. And there were a couple of times where I – I swear I saw her up ahead of me. Sitting in a little rowing boat, bobbing on the water. Her hair… And she was like laughing, you know the way she laughs?

DONAL *listens*.

I even called out once or twice, called her name but then… wasn't her. Just buoys or marks or whatever. And then… well then I couldn't help thinking about Dad. Out there on his own in the middle of the night, the waves battering the side of his boat. Wearing him down. And I thought – fuck, must have been lonely. Must've been lonely to die out there like that… with no one knowing.

He takes a swig of beer.

'Cept of course *she* knew. She let him go out, whatever she says. She did… Or maybe he's not out there at all. Maybe the two of you have him buried here under the patio?

DONAL. Don't be fucking stupid.

COLM. You wouldn't tell me anyway.

DONAL. You think she could hide a body for ten years and then when it suits her have it moved to the patio?

COLM. Unless it was there all along…

DONAL. You honestly think she'd be capable of that?

COLM. I honestly think Beiv's capable of anything.

Beat.

You know I'm almost sure I can remember her putting me in a dress and sending me to school.

DONAL. Almost sure.

COLM. Like I can hear her in my head, saying – saying she didn't want to me to be stifled by my gender. Or something.

DONAL. Could be considered progressive now.

COLM. Not then. Then it was fucked up. But I suppose this whole thing is fucked up isn't it? I'm fucked up… you're fucked up.

DONAL *looks up, sharp*.

DONAL. I'm not fucked up… And you know what? I actually resent you for saying that.

COLM *glances at him*.

COLM. Okay… sorry.

DONAL. You're not though. And you're not sorry for what you said yesterday either.

COLM. What did I say yesterday?

DONAL. That you blame me for what happened the other night.

COLM. Ah look /

DONAL. You said it.

COLM. Can we not do this right now?

DONAL. *You* were the one who grabbed my crotch. *You* were the one who unzipped *my* jeans. *You* were the one who wanted to fuck –

COLM. I was drunk.

DONAL. That's honestly your excuse?

COLM. I didn't see you putting up any arguments.

DONAL. Of course I didn't put up any arguments. Why would I put up any arguments? I've been in love with you since I was sixteen years old.

COLM *stops, surprised*.

I ruined my fucking life for you, Colm. Not that it's ever occurred to you.

COLM. I don't even know what we're talking about here.

DONAL. Really? You really have that little notion of what it's like to be the one left waiting?

COLM. When were you left waiting?

DONAL. You'd just swan down here every summer with your fancy artist family and my little world would just light up. Just light fucking up for the few weeks I had you with me... then you'd fuck back off up to Dublin again and I wouldn't hear from you for six months, a year. But I didn't mind. I knew you'd be back next summer. And I knew when you came back, you'd want to see me, because you *always* wanted to see me. And that's just the way it was.

COLM. We were teenagers, Donal.

DONAL. Yeah. We were... but then that first winter of college you ring me up out of the blue and say you miss me. Say you need to see me, like urgently, like you're going to fucking die if you don't.

COLM. No I /

DONAL. And I drop everything, classes everything, to come down here and spend a week with you.

COLM. My parents had split up, I'd just started college.

DONAL. You said you loved me.

COLM. I was confused.

DONAL. I left my degree and came to Dublin because of what you said.

COLM. Well I never asked you to.

DONAL. Yes you did... You just didn't like it when I actually did it. Because at that stage, you'd gone and made yourself some friends, found a scene, didn't need me any more.

COLM. Okay look /

DONAL. Some fucking culchie from the summer holidays following you around.

COLM. I wasn't ready, okay?

They look at one another.

...I wasn't like you.

DONAL. Well you seemed pretty like me that week in this house. You seemed pretty like me the other night in that field, or all the other times over the years you couldn't wait to see my cock.

COLM. I didn't love you, alright... The way that you loved me. I didn't. And I'm sorry if that's – hurtful or whatever but it's just a fact.

DONAL. So it was just sex?

COLM. No. No it wasn't just sex...

DONAL. You could fuck me but you didn't want to go out with me, is that it? The idea of a relationship just turned your stomach?

COLM. Yes actually it kind of did.

DONAL *steps back, wounded.*

COLM *rubs his eyes, stressed.*

Why are we even talking about this? It was *so* long ago Donal, I mean haven't we moved on?

DONAL. It was the other night.

COLM. But aren't there more important things happening right now? My wife being fucking missing for one.

DONAL. Or your parents splitting up, or your mom meeting another woman or your dad –

COLM. Disappearing at sea? (*Voice rising.*) Yes! This is my messed-up life, I'm sorry if it's inconvenient.

DONAL. You have never taken any risks.

COLM. What?

DONAL. You have no idea what it's like to be a kid in a place like this and be different.

COLM. Oh for fuck's sake, Donal, it's the twenty-first century, gays could not be more celebrated now, especially here – where they voted for you to get fucking married. People like *you* are not victims any more.

DONAL. People like me?

COLM. I know you want to be, but you're not. It's over.

DONAL....Easy for you to say.

DONAL *stares at him, disgust.*

COLM *takes a deep breath, tries to steady himself.*

COLM. Look... you were good to me, Donal. At a time, at *times* when I really needed someone to be good to me. You were... and yes we had a sexual – connection and yes we still have it, I can't explain it but it's there – you're right, it's there... But you and me?... that's never going to happen. It's not what I wanted for my life or my future or – ever. And I'm sorry about that. I'm really sorry if I gave you the wrong impression *when we were kids, Donal.* But I don't know how I can be any more explicit. I don't want to be with you like that. I never did.

DONAL....except in the dark.

COLM *looks at him. Shrugs. He has no more answers.*

Beat.

You know when I came up to Dublin that time – after leaving my course and everything and you said – well basically you said the same thing you've said just now... Beiv was the one who took me in.

COLM *looks up, surprised.*

I didn't have anywhere to go, see, cos I didn't actually know anyone in Dublin, apart from ye. So the only person I could think to call, was Beiv. She'd just come back from whatever shit she'd been doing down here, and had gotten herself a flat in Ringsend. She told me to come straight over. So I did. Stayed a few months actually. Got a job in a bar. You weren't speaking to her, you didn't know... She begged me to go back to college. Begged me not to throw my life away over 'a man', she said. Said I should think of the bigger picture. 'Someday you'll look back on this and it'll mean nothing,' that's what she said.

He looks at COLM.

Funny how all this time's gone by… and that's still not true.

Beat.

Anyway, I am going back. To finish my degree. I'm going to London this September. Got a place and everything.

COLM *looks up*.

COLM. That's – great.

DONAL *nods*.

No, that's really –

DONAL. Beiv's paying for it.

COLM*'s visibly taken aback*.

Fees, accommodation, the lot. She's paying for it.

Beat.

She told me not to tell you… It's the money from the house. Your – cut of the money from the house. That you threw back in her face. She's giving it to me, to study.

COLM. She didn't waste much time… I'd be careful. She'll want something for that.

DONAL. She says you owe it to me.

COLM. Oh yeah?

DONAL. You *do* owe it to me.

Beat.

COLM. Well, she's always liked you more than she liked me.

DONAL. She loved your old man, too. In her way.

COLM. Yeah right.

DONAL. You know I don't think you can properly remember what he was like. He used drive you crazy. His silences. His moods – you couldn't wait to get away.

COLM. He wasn't always like that. Only after they split.

DONAL. That week we came down here, and he found us in bed, remember how he laid into you?

COLM *frowns*.

COLM. No.

DONAL. Do you not remember?

COLM. Not really.

COLM *shakes his head*.

DONAL. He dragged you outside in your boxers, held you up against that wall and he was screaming into your face. Just screaming and screaming. Everyone round here would've heard… And don't get me wrong, like, I liked old Mike. I didn't blame him for being – angry. Wasn't about us anyway. Don't think he even cared about that bit. He was just so freaked out that you'd run off without telling him… But the way he was, screaming and hitting you, I was fucking terrified. Terrified for you.

COLM *takes this in*.

COLM. Well he pushed things down… do it myself sometimes. I just bottle it and bottle it and take it and take it. And then something happens and it all comes out in one stupid – explosion, like with Bonnie the other night. And then I hate myself even more. You know?

Beat.

Maybe I am like him in that way. Do you think?

He looks at DONAL, *genuine*.

Do you think I have that – darkness just waiting inside me?

DONAL *shrugs*.

DONAL.…I think I've spent far too much time thinking about your pain, Colm. I think it's probably about time I thought of myself for a bit. You know?

Beat.

COLM *nods*.

DONAL *looks at his watch*.

I'm going home to get some kip… if she's not back in another few hours we need to get the guards.

COLM. I know.

> DONAL *heads for the door. Suddenly* COLM *grabs his hand –*

I'm afraid, Donal.

> DONAL *looks at him.*

I'm afraid of what they're going to find.

DONAL....I know.

> DONAL *resists the urge to hold him.*

But whatever it is, you'll face it. You're strong like that.

> *He removes his hand from* COLM*'s.*

> *He goes to the door.*

See ya.

> DONAL *goes.*

> COLM *watches after him.*

COLM. See ya, Donal.

Eight

Mid-afternoon the next day.

Voices outside the cottage, the door handle turns and opens.

RAY, *a hipster type, skinny jeans, beard, a hat, enters.*

He looks around.

RAY. Oh my fucking god.

> BONNIE *steps into the house behind him.*

> *She's wearing the same clothes we last saw her in but has a man's jacket thrown around her shoulders for warmth.*

> RAY *smiles at her.*

Oh my fucking god, this is incredible.

BONNIE. I know, right?

RAY. She seriously never locks the place?

BONNIE. Nope.

RAY. It's exactly how I imagined.

He walks to the large painting on the easel, touches it.

This is hers yeah?

BONNIE. That's my favourite of her new ones.

RAY. Wow.

He takes out his phone, starts to take a picture.

BONNIE (*worried*). Hey – what are you doing?

RAY. Oh, it's just /

BONNIE. You can't take pictures.

RAY. It's just for my records. I'm not gonna show anyone.

BONNIE. You can't put them up anywhere. Like online or anything?

RAY. No no, course not. It's just for me. Promise.

He squeezes her hand, slightly intimate.

Shit, look at those skulls.

RAY *goes to the table with the skulls.*

BONNIE. They're just for sketches.

RAY. So she says.

He takes a picture of the skulls.

BONNIE. Hey, give me that.

She grabs the phone.

RAY. What?

BONNIE (*worried*). You're not going to sell these or anything?

RAY. No, god.

BONNIE. Cos we had a deal.

RAY. I know.

He reaches for the phone. She holds it away.

BONNIE. I just said I'd show you the house.

RAY. I'm not gonna show anyone, I swear.

BONNIE. She could sue you.

RAY. It's just to help me remember. Bit of background detail, that's all. I've spent a year trying to get into this place, I don't want to forget.

He reaches for the phone.

She lets him take it.

He smiles at her, moves away.

She watches him, less trusting now.

He gestures to the window.

What happened here?

BONNIE *looks.*

BONNIE. I don't know.

RAY *takes a picture of it.*

RAY. Probably one of the neighbours.

BONNIE. Why would one of the neighbours do it?

RAY. Why wouldn't they?

BONNIE. She's not bothering anyone.

RAY. Think how you'd feel, living your life on some quiet little island, some egomaniac artist decides to start a commune.

BONNIE. That was years ago.

RAY. And it pissed people off.

BONNIE. How do you know?

RAY. I've talked to them.

BONNIE. The neighbours?

RAY. Some, yeah. You should hear some of the shit that went down. Orgies… she even punched a woman.

BONNIE. At an orgy?

RAY. No, but like… it was mad.

BONNIE *shakes her head.*

BONNIE. Well I don't think she did it.

RAY. That's cos you're sweet.

RAY *starts taking pictures of the furniture.*

BONNIE. It just doesn't make sense to me, the whole 'staged sailing accident' thing…

RAY. Makes sense to me.

BONNIE. It's stupid.

RAY. There are people who saw her that night. Rowing back to the harbour.

BONNIE. People who were drunk.

RAY. Next day they find his boat out past the beacon.

BONNIE. So what – she dragged his body onto a boat, then sailed out to sea making it look like an accident, before rowing herself back to dry land.

RAY. She could've have killed him out there.

BONNIE. I don't buy it.

RAY. Look facts are facts. She was the last person with him. She has no alibi, she has no explanation for why he went out so late at night and he left her everything. Literally every penny.

BONNIE. They were friends.

RAY. She did it. You said yourself the son even thinks so.

BONNIE *looks away.*

Hey, do you think he'd give me an interview?

BONNIE. Who?

RAY. The son.

BONNIE. No.

RAY. But like – would you know him well enough to ask?

BONNIE. Not really.

RAY's disappointed.

RAY. I'm not trying to pressure you. I just thought, given you
seem to know them –

BONNIE (*firm*). I wouldn't feel comfortable about that.

RAY. Okay. Cool.

RAY backs off.

That's – cool. I'm just asking.

RAY touches her face.

No need to look so anxious.

Maybe he gives her a little kiss.

BONNIE *moves away.*

I should record something.

BONNIE. Record?

RAY. Hang on.

He takes out his phone, presses the record button

(*Into phone.*) I'm standing in the cottage that's now owned
by Beiv Scanlon –

BONNIE. What are you –

He gestures for her to keep quiet.

RAY. The last place Michael Scanlon was seen alive.

He pauses the recording.

Radio's actually a really visual medium, so you have to set
the scene. Paint a picture in the listener's mind, you know, so
they can really – see it.

He unpauses the recording. BONNIE *glances at him, a touch warily, then moves into the kitchen.*

On one hand it looks like an idyllic little artist's garret. Half-finished charcoal sketches sit scattered on a table. A large oil painting rests on an easel, there's a huge glass window with sweeping views of the Atlantic. But the crack in the window from a recent break-in, suggests another story. A darker story… a story of sex and violence and betrayal that's hung around this cottage for over a / decade –

DONAL *enters in his overalls. He stops.*

DONAL. Who the fuck are you?

RAY *whirls round, turns off the recorder.*

RAY. Oh hey hey… (*Calling.*) Bonnie!

BONNIE *comes out of the kitchen.*

BONNIE. Hi, Donal.

DONAL *looks at her, surprised.*

DONAL. Bonnie! Shit – when did you get back?

BONNIE. Just now.

DONAL. Colm and Beiv've just taken the ferry over to the guards.

BONNIE. Is that where they were going? I saw them get on it…

DONAL. You didn't stop them?

BONNIE. They didn't see me.

She looks at RAY.

This is Ray by the way. Ray, this is Donal. He's a family friend of… the family.

RAY. Hey, man, how are you?

DONAL *glances at him, perfunctory. Looks back at* BONNIE.

DONAL. We should call them. Let them know you're okay.

DONAL *takes out his phone.*

BONNIE. Ray's producing the podcast.

DONAL *looks up.*

DONAL.… What?

BONNIE. I've been telling him it's all bullshit. Beiv didn't kill anyone but –

RAY. Yeah she's been really trying to convince me. But come on…

DONAL (*to* BONNIE). What the fuck? Are you crazy?

RAY. Hey – don't speak to her like that.

DONAL (*to* RAY). Get out of this house.

RAY. Look, man, I'm not here to cause any trouble –

DONAL. Just get out.

RAY. She invited me.

DONAL. Well she doesn't have the authority to do that.

RAY. And you do?

DONAL. Yes. Now get the fuck out.

DONAL *gives him a shove towards the door.*

RAY. Hey /

BONNIE. He just took a few pictures.

DONAL. What?

RAY (*nervous*). No I – Bonnie –

DONAL. What pictures? With what?

BONNIE. They're on his phone.

RAY. Bonnie…

DONAL *looks at* RAY.

DONAL. Give me your phone.

RAY. Look can we just relax here for a second –

DONAL. Give me the fucking phone.

RAY. It's my journalistic privilege to protect my /

DONAL *suddenly slams* RAY *against the wall*.

DONAL. Jesus fucking Christ. Give it to me! /

DONAL *shoves his hand into* RAY*'s pocket, they struggle*.

RAY. Hey! You can't do that.

DONAL *retrieves the phone*.

That's got all my research.

DONAL. I don't give a fuck what it's got on it. It's not leaving this house.

DONAL *grabs something, a poker, a hammer.* RAY *watches, panicked –*

RAY. What are you – what are you doing?

DONAL *starts smashing the phone over and over again*.

Shit, man! You can't do that.

DONAL *keeps hitting it*.

That's my property. (*To* BONNIE.) I'm getting the cops…

DONAL *turns*.

DONAL. Yeah and while you're at it, you can tell them all about how you were breaking and entering /

RAY. You're a lunatic.

DONAL *grabs* RAY *by the arm, pushes him towards the door.*

DONAL. And if you come back near this house again, I swear that'll be your fucking head where that phone is. You hear me? You hear me!

DONAL *throws* RAY *out*.

He slams the door.

Fucking parasite.

BONNIE *stares at* DONAL.

Silence.

DONAL *picks up the smashed phone. He looks at it, then at* BONNIE.

Where the hell have you been?

BONNIE. Nowhere. Here.

DONAL. We've combed every inch of this island looking for you, Bonnie.

She pulls the coat around herself.

BONNIE. This place is wild… I met some people, camping. Stayed out drinking with them one of the nights… they had a boat so the next day we went to one of the islands. That's where I met Ray.

DONAL. The fucking Scorsese of podcasts?

BONNIE. He's okay.

DONAL. Well Colm's been worried sick. He was out in the boat all night last night looking for you.

BONNIE.…And the night before, he was with you.

DONAL *stops.*

BONNIE. Guess he's been pretty busy.

She looks up at DONAL, *almost smiles.*

You look so freaked out right now… What – you guys thought I just took off for no reason?

DONAL. No. We thought – we thought that maybe you were upset after – the other night, with Colm.

BONNIE. Yeah I was. I was really upset. We've never fought like that before. I went back to our room to calm down. And then I started to feel bad, like I'd been really – unnecessarily hysterical or something and embarrassed Colm in front of everybody. So I walked back up here to apologise and on the way… I saw the two of you.

DONAL. We'd had a lot to drink.

BONNIE. You don't need to explain.

DONAL. Well –

BONNIE. Colm's told me all about you.

DONAL (*taken aback*). Oh… what did he say?

BONNIE. That you were his first. How important that was.

DONAL. He said that?

BONNIE. Well, no. Actually he said it wasn't that important at all, but I don't believe him. Everyone's first is important.

Beat.

Actually, I always thought it was pretty cool that he was so easy and open about his history. Cos most guys… And sexuality *is* fluid, I do think that. And monogamy is *hard*. I always said if it came to it, maybe we could have an open relationship – if that's what we wanted, you know if that's what worked. Why not? I'm not a jealous person.

She looks at him.

But then I saw you both together the other night and it sort of… broke me.

Beat.

Cos I realised – it's all bullshit. I just want Colm to myself. I want him all to myself, I'm his wife.

DONAL. I know. /

BONNIE. That's my right.

DONAL. I know /

BONNIE. He's *mine*. I should be the one to save him, not you. *Fuck you.*

DONAL *is stunned by her ferocity.*

I am not an idiot!

Tears stream down BONNIE*'s face.*

She tries to wipe them away, gather herself.

DONAL. I never thought that you were.

Beat.

BONNIE. You know my family are actually just really – boring people. Who want me to have a nice, happy life. And I've always hated them for it. For being so conventional, cos *this* is what I wanted – this. Something *interesting* and artistic and… God.

She'd laugh if she wasn't about to cry.

And you know, I thought that in not judging Colm's past or not judging his family or whatever, I was seeing him in a way that no one else could see him. I was accepting him for who he was, totally and completely. I thought I was *so* important… but I'm not.

DONAL. There's nothing between me and Colm, Bonnie.

BONNIE. That's patently not true.

DONAL. Well it's not going any further so –

BONNIE. So I should just relax? Cos it's all fine?

DONAL. No. I'm not saying… look things got out of hand the other night.

BONNIE. Yeah –

DONAL. And I apologise for my part in that. It's confused me as much as you, believe me.

She looks at him.

But for what it's worth like, I do think Colm – genuinely loves you.

BONNIE. Why?

DONAL. Cos… he wants it to work between ye.

BONNIE. That doesn't mean he loves me.

DONAL. Well he wants it to work between ye in a way he never wanted it to work with me for example. He didn't choose me.

Beat.

BONNIE....Did you choose him?

DONAL....Yeah.

BONNIE takes this in.

BONNIE. That sucks.

DONAL. It does, yeah.

Silence.

BONNIE. But is that enough? To be chosen? When you've already been betrayed?

DONAL. Yeah, I don't... that's for yourselves to sort out really, isn't it?

BONNIE. I guess.

She looks around. Her gaze rests on the skulls.

She gets up and walks towards them.

Ray's taking the ferry later. To interview some true-crime fanatics on the mainland. They've all these crazy theories about Beiv.

DONAL. Fucking parasites. People that feed off that shit.

BONNIE. I don't think they mean any harm.

DONAL. Still –

BONNIE. It's just not real to them. That's all.

DONAL. Like the people who come down here every summer. Who drink and swim and pretend they're like us. They're not like us. They're on fucking holidays.

BONNIE. Like me, you mean?

DONAL. No. Not you.

BONNIE....Like Colm?

He looks at her.

DONAL. Maybe a bit like Colm, yeah.

BONNIE manages a little smile.

People who don't see what they do to other people.

BONNIE *turns back to the skulls*.

BONNIE....I think I'm gonna go with Ray. On the ferry.

DONAL (*surprised*). What – now?

BONNIE nods.

BONNIE. He's offered to show me the sights. Says he'll drive me anywhere I want to go.

She looks at him, dry.

Might as well see some of the countryside.

DONAL. But what about Colm? You have to tell him you're alright.

BONNIE. You can tell him.

DONAL. No you should talk to him. Here – we'll call them.

BONNIE (*forceful*). No!

DONAL stops.

I don't know what I want to say. Yet.

DONAL. So like… when should I tell him you'll be back?

BONNIE thinks.

BONNIE. Tell him I'll see him at the airport.

DONAL. The airport?

BONNIE. Tell him he can text me if he wants. I'll text back, but I'll see him at the airport.

Beat.

I'm gonna get my things out of our room.

DONAL. Okay.

She looks at the skull again.

BONNIE. This really isn't how I pictured my honeymoon in Ireland.

DONAL. No, I can imagine…

Life's full of little surprises, isn't it.

They look at one another.

A strange sadness hangs between them.

BONNIE.... Yeah... it is.

Nine

Evening. The next day.

COLM *paces in front of the window, phone to his ear.*

He moves from pleading to anger and back.

COLM. Bonnie – Bonnie, just listen... I'm not, I swear I'm
    not... I'm worried... About you... but you don't know
    that... No you don't, you don't, Bonnie... I know but –

    BEIV *comes in the front door carrying two brown bags of
    fish and chips.*

    She glances at COLM, *goes to the kitchen.*

    I won't, I promise... I won't... I won't... Just tell me where
    you are, Bonnie... Cos I'm worried. I can't just sit here and
    fucking –

    He tries to stay calm, gentle.

    Please, Bonnie – come on, Bonnie – Just tell me where
    you... I *won't*... Please, just tell me where you are... Please
    just tell me where you are... Please just –

    She hangs up.

    COLM *stands, staring at the phone in his hand.*

    BEIV *comes out with the brown bags now on two plates. She
    hands him one.*

BEIV. Don't tell me. She didn't tell you.

COLM. She's out near Bantry or somewhere.

BEIV. Well she's fine then.

COLM. With him.

BEIV. The podcast fella?

COLM. Think she's fucking him.

BEIV. Did she say that?

COLM. Well not explicitly, no. But they've been sleeping in his car.

BEIV. ...Oh.

COLM. What does that mean? 'Oh.'

BEIV *sits*

BEIV. Means you're probably right.

COLM. Ah Jesus, don't agree with me. I don't want you agreeing with me.

BEIV. What? You can hardly blame the girl. Actually I think fair play to her. She's got more gumption than I gave her credit for.

COLM. Okay. Stop. I'm seeing her at the airport, we'll sort it out then.

COLM *sits down and tears open the chip bag.*

He stuffs some chips into his mouth.

BEIV. It's better that she gets it out of her system.

COLM. Beiv.

BEIV. Then at least you're even. Better to be even. Nothing worse than being the one who has to be forgiven over and over.

COLM. Well you'd know.

BEIV. Exactly.

He looks at her.

They eat.

COLM *gestures to the window.*

COLM. When are they coming to fix that?

BEIV. I dunno. One in the kitchen's still covered with cardboard, that really bothers me. That one –

She gestures to the crack.

I actually sort of like.

COLM. It's in keeping with the place anyway. And your little piece of live performance art.

BEIV looks up surprised.

Letting them all see in here.

BEIV smiles.

BEIV. Is that what I'm doing?

BEIV gestures the painting on the easel.

…Been meaning to move that out of the way.

COLM. Why?

BEIV. When it's just sitting there it's too tempting to keep going at it.

COLM. So it's finished?

BEIV. I don't know. I never know when something's finished. Your father used to be the one to tell me.

COLM (*surprised*). Dad?

BEIV. He'd come to the studio and say – 'Leave that now, that's done. If you go at it any more, you'll only ruin it.'

COLM. And was he right?

BEIV. Most of the time.

COLM. Mad really, that a solicitor could have such a feeling for art.

BEIV. Well he wasn't just a solicitor… no more than you're just a software engineer.

COLM. Don't.

BEIV. What?

COLM. I'm very happy to be a software engineer.

BEIV. I know.

COLM. We don't all need to be artists to be special. In fact, better not to think you're special at all. Better to just be… and that is not a blood orange.

BEIV *looks at the painting, surprised.*

BEIV. How do you know?

COLM. Cos it doesn't look like a blood orange.

BEIV. Oh come on. You might reject everything I stand for but I know you know what abstract art is.

COLM. Yeah, a cop-out.

BEIV. Why is it a cop-out?

COLM. Cos it can never be wrong. You look at a literal picture of a blood orange and you think 'yeah that's a convincing blood orange.' Or 'no, that's bullshit. That's a really shitty blood orange. This person has no talent.' You look at that and you can see whatever you want.

BEIV. And that's a problem why?

COLM. It's just a bit 'one for everyone in the audience', isn't it?

BEIV. And what about Chagall? You've always liked him, he's anything but literal.

COLM. Well he's a real artist.

Beat.

BEIV. Okay.

Beat.

So what do you see when you look at that?

He shrugs, eating.

COLM. Nothing. Splodges. I literally just see splodges.

BEIV. Because that's what you want to see. Because everyone sees what they want to see.

He shakes his head.

Including the police.

COLM. No the police think we're fucking nutjobs. They think we're addicted to reporting people missing.

BEIV. Well I'd love to have seen their faces when Bonnie turned up.

They smile.

COLM. Maybe it'll work in your favour.

BEIV. What? That I reported my daughter-in-law missing and then found her a few hours later.

COLM. It's a twist…

BEIV. Does it make me look more innocent or more guilty?

COLM. Makes you look like a crazy old bat.

BEIV. Well, I am.

They laugh.

They stop.

They keep eating.

COLM *(quietly)*. I'm sorry for what I said the other… for calling you a liar.

BEIV.…That's alright.

A beat.

COLM. What happened that night, Beiv? With Dad?

BEIV. You know what happened.

COLM. Not really.

BEIV. I've told you a million times.

COLM. You haven't, actually. No, I don't think you have. Other people have told me and you've responded to things they've said, but you haven't actually told me yourself. In your own words. Not in a long time.

BEIV. Do I have to do it now?

Beat.

COLM. Donal says I don't remember what he was like. That he
was – harder or darker than I remember him.

BEIV. We're all selective about our dead.

COLM. But was he ever... like did he ever do anything to you
that I didn't know about?

BEIV. Like what?

COLM. I don't know. Donal seemed to think he was violent.

BEIV. No.

COLM. He was violent with me.

BEIV. That time you came down here? He was beside himself.

COLM. But was he ever violent with you? You had some
almighty rows. He never hit you or hurt you or –

BEIV. Did anything to give me a motive to kill him? No. He did
not.

Beat.

He was my very best friend.

COLM. But is there anything I don't know?

BEIV. About Michael? I'm sure there's lots.

COLM. But is there anything I *should* know? I'm getting on
a plane in a few days, I might not be back till –

BEIV. I'm dead? You wish.

COLM. I don't know is the point. I don't know when I'll be back.
Cos I'll go back to my life there with Bonnie – I hope – and
work and that will consume me and this will recede and...

He takes a breath.

You don't know what's it's like when you've lived somewhere
else for a long time. The place you came from just stays as it
was in your head. Exactly as it was when you left. And you

come back years later thinking it'll all be the same. I mean you
know it won't, rationally, but you also think it will. People will
be the same, food will be the same, the same shops will be in
the same places and when they're not – it's kind of a shock…
Sometimes people have died. Sometimes shops have changed
or been knocked down and it's stupid cos you were the one
who left in the first place, but suddenly you feel – unmoored.
Like you don't know who you are any more. Like everyone
you love has just gone and moved house and no one has told
you. It's like a – a grief. Or something – I fucking dread that
feeling… So if there's something that might help me feel – not
so left behind, next time, I'd be grateful if you told me. If
there's something about Dad I don't know – and I think there
is, I really think there is, Beiv… I'd like you to tell me. Now.

BEIV *looks at him for a long time*.

BEIV. He thought he killed someone.

COLM.…Dad?

BEIV *nods*.

BEIV. When he was a child.

COLM. He thought – who did he think he killed?

BEIV. Nuala O'Neill's little boy.

COLM (*shocked*). What?

BEIV. I don't remember his name. Isn't that strange?

COLM.…how?

BEIV *shrugs*.

BEIV. They were out in some boats one day fishing and the
little boy was drowned.

COLM. And Dad thought – he did it?

BEIV. Michael was around twelve I think. The O'Neill boy
was a year or so younger. He was a spoiled kid. Only child.
Michael and his friends didn't like him. They didn't like
the way he tagged on or told tales or squealed or whatever.
You know, kids. But they were always made to play with

him by the parents so… one day they were out in a boat and they were out quite far and they – I don't know for a joke or something they must've pushed him into the water. Or they threw something into the water and dared him to jump in and get it, which he did. And when he tried to swim back and get onto the boat, they got this idea to keep pushing him back in. There were five or six of them, one of him, so he was outnumbered. But he kept trying to get back into the boat and the lads kept pushing him back into the water and some of them were pushing his head down. Michael was one of them. He said he distinctly remembered the black of the boy's hair under his hand. And his pale face, coming up and coughing, before someone'd push him back under again. And even when it was clear he was getting tired and they should stop… they didn't want to stop. They were having so much fun, pushing him back and holding him down for longer and longer stretches until eventually… he went limp.

Beat.

Course they pulled him into the boat straight away, tried to give him mouth-to-mouth but he was white as a sheet. They got him back to land and ran for a doctor and Nuala O'Neill was on the beach howling. And the boys all said it was an accident, told anyone who'd listen that he'd swallowed too much water. And the police came and there was a post mortem and the person who did it said – it was to do with his heart. He had a defect or something and it gave out. But Michael and his friends knew the truth. Some of the parents knew it too but they told their kids to shut up, that they'd only get themselves in trouble. There was no appetite locally for punishment. Most of them convinced themselves it *was* his heart. Maybe it was… but Michael didn't think so.

A silence.

COLM. Is that true?

BEIV. What do you mean?

COLM. Like – you're not making that up?

BEIV. Of course I'm not making it up.

COLM. So why have you never told me that before?

BEIV. Michael asked me not to.

COLM. But he told you?

BEIV. Yes.

COLM. When?

BEIV. Loads of times.

COLM. But when first?

BEIV. I don't know. When we were going out?

COLM. Before you were married?

BEIV. Yes.

COLM.…And you didn't think he was a fucking disgrace?

BEIV. I didn't think he did what he thought he did. And neither did he back then – he thought it was an accident, like the rest of them. It was only much much later, when you were a – teenager in fact, that it started getting to him.

COLM. When I was a teenager? What are you –

BEIV. The image of the boy's black hair under his hand. And the thrill.

COLM. The thrill?

BEIV. That's what he said… And watching you grow up… he couldn't stop thinking about it. It would flash into his head in the street, or when he was in the middle of talking to someone, it would catch him in his chest and he couldn't breathe…

COLM. Like a panic attack?

BEIV. Yes.

COLM. He started having panic attacks?

BEIV. Went on for years.

COLM. And did he see someone about it?

BEIV. Like who?

COLM. A doctor.

BEIV. The only person he could talk to about it was me. Cos I was the only person he'd ever told. And we talked about it a lot. Even after the separation. Sometimes he'd ring me in the middle of the night and we would talk, for hours until he felt able to hang up the phone. I didn't mind talking to him but after a while, after years and years, it got so bad that talking wasn't doing any good. Talking was making it worse, so…

COLM. So what?

BEIV. I think he just wanted it to stop.

COLM *looks at her.*

COLM. So that's what he was doing going out in the boat that night? Making it stop?

BEIV. …it's possible.

Beat.

COLM. You never said that to the police.

BEIV. I said he was depressed. I've always said that.

COLM. But did he tell you that? Did he specifically tell you he was going out in the boat that night to make it stop? Cos if he did, you should have stopped him. He was obviously having some kind of psychotic –

BEIV. It was real to him.

COLM. No.

BEIV. There was nothing anyone could've said.

COLM. Yes there was.

BEIV. *He was suffering.*

COLM *stares at her.*

COLM. So he did tell you.

BEIV *looks down.*

Or were you actually out in the boat with him? Like all those people said you were. Maybe you thought he *should* do it –

BEIV *shakes her head.*

Or maybe he just didn't want to be alone. Maybe he asked you to be with him. Is what happened? What happened?

BEIV *closes her eyes.*

Did you do it for him, Beiv? Hold his head under the water? I mean we know he was weak. We know you're so much stronger. Maybe he chickened out. Maybe he asked you to put him out of his misery – like an animal? I'm sure you could do that, Beiv. I'm sure you have that in you. Is that what happened? What happened, Beiv? What happened to my father that night?

BEIV *opens her eyes, looks at him.*

BEIV. It won't change anything to know.

Beat.

I'm the one who has to live with it. I owed him that.

COLM. Jesus Christ. Jesus fucking…

COLM *stops.*

How do I know you haven't made all this up?

BEIV. Why would I do that?

COLM. To cover for yourself. To turn me against his memory.

BEIV. I don't want to turn you against his memory.

COLM. Do you think he killed that little boy?

BEIV. I don't know.

COLM. Cos it sounds like it could've been an accident.

BEIV. It could have been.

COLM. It sounds like he *could've* had a heart condition.

BEIV. Yes.

COLM. So maybe the truth is Dad didn't actually do anything. Maybe it was all in his head. Cos he was sick. And he should have got help. Or maybe he just felt bad about that boy because he had a conscience?

BEIV. We're never going to know.

COLM. But I want to know. I want to know the truth.

BEIV. The only truth we know, is that he thought that he did.

Silence.

Eventually BEIV *reaches for his plate.*

Are you done here?

He gives her his plate.

COLM. I want to get out of here.

Beat.

I want to get out of this place and I never want to come back.

BEIV. I understand that.

COLM. The only thing you and I ever had in common was Dad.

BEIV. That's not true.

COLM. Yes it is. You have always loved your – art far more than you have ever loved me.

BEIV. I just found it more satisfying. That's all.

COLM *takes this in.*

BEIV *goes into the kitchen. We hear her put down the plates.*

COLM *looks up at the painting.*

BEIV *comes back in.*

When you got over your fear of boats, and went out sailing by yourself for the first time, I was so proud. So proud. Not for any woolly 'feel the fear and do it anyway' reason. But because for the first time, you were ruthless. The way an artist has to be ruthless – to cut off the rest world and dig in on what it is they want to say. And you did. You cut the fear right out of yourself that day and you went out to sea, not because the other boys were doing it, but because you knew if you didn't, your life was not your own. And you were right. And I was proud. I *am* proud. Your victories are all your own. Your father and I made our choices, but they are not yours to carry… I'm not afraid of planes, Colm. I just want you to be free. Free of me, free of your father, free of anything you don't need. You are free.

He looks at her.

COLM. And what if I go to the police?

BEIV *stands very still.*

BEIV.…Then that's your choice.

COLM. And what if I walk out that door tomorrow and never come back?

BEIV. I'll know that you made the right one.

They look at one another.

Then COLM *turns back and stares up at the painting.*

COLM. I still just see splodges.

He starts to point.

Splodges of red. And splodges of purple. And splodges of pink. And splodges of green. And splodges of yellow. And splodges of grey. And splodges of blue. And splodges of white.

BEIV *stands in the doorway listening.*

And splodges of crimson. And splodges of magenta. And splodges of turquoise. And splodges of sea. And splodges of land. And splodges of trees. And splodges of tears. And splodges of hair. Splodges of black hair… And a hand…

He stops.

Lights down.

The End.

Druid

Druid was founded in Galway in 1975 by Garry Hynes, Marie Mullen and Mick Lally, the first professional Irish theatre company outside of Dublin.

Druid has a rich history of presenting award-winning productions and event theatre of established playwrights and popular classics all over the world. The company's successes include *The Beauty Queen of Leenane*, in a co-production with the Royal Court Theatre, which went on to win four Tony Awards, including Best Director for Garry Hynes, the first woman to win an award for directing in the history of the Tony Awards; *The Leenane Trilogy* (with the Royal Court); *DruidSynge* – all six John Millington Synge plays in a single day; *DruidMurphy* – Plays by Tom Murphy, a trilogy of *Conversations on a Homecoming*, *A Whistle in the Dark* and *Famine*; *DruidShakespeare* – *Richard II*, *Henry IV (Pts. 1&2)*, *Henry V* in a new adaptation by Mark O'Rowe; and *Waiting for Godot* by Samuel Beckett.

Druid is a writers' theatre with a long track record for premiering new plays of international stature. The company has premiered many productions, among them: *Conversations on a Homecoming* and *Bailegangáire* by Tom Murphy, *The Beauty Queen of Leenane* and *The Lonesome West* by Martin McDonagh, *The Walworth Farce* and *The New Electric Ballroom* by Enda Walsh, and *My Brilliant Divorce* by Geraldine Aron.

The Gate Theatre

The Gate Theatre is an iconic Dublin theatre of world-class excellence led by Director Selina Cartmell. Founded in 1928 by the visionary artists Hilton Edwards and Micheál MacLiammóir, the Gate's groundbreaking productions are innovative and experimental, offering audiences important work from European and American theatre, alongside classics from the modern and Irish repertoire.

Under the directorship of Michael Colgan during the 1990s, the Gate mounted international festivals of the work of Samuel Beckett, Brian Friel and Harold Pinter. Orson Welles, James Mason, Geraldine Fitzgerald and Michael Gambon began their acting careers at the Gate.

Recent successes include commissioning Roddy Doyle's sold-out production of *The Snapper* for the stage, the immersive production of F. Scott Fitzgerald's *The Great Gatsby*, and Ruth Negga's acclaimed performance in the title role in *Hamlet*. New writing is cultivated and valued, with commissions for such talented Irish writers as Nancy Harris and Emmett Kirwan, and productions of plays by contemporary dramatists such as Lucy Kirkwood, Nina Raine and David Eldridge.

Selina Cartmell's appointment in 2017 was described in the *Guardian* as 'a new dawn for the theatre'. A commitment to representation and diversity, reinvigorating classic texts, and creating relevant new work are at the forefront of her artistic vision.

www.nickhernbooks.co.uk

 facebook.com/nickhernbooks

 twitter.com/nickhernbooks